DBT

WORKBOOK FOR KIDS

**The Friendly and Practical Dialectical Behavior
Therapy Skills Training for Emotional Regulation and
Self-Care**

Payton Black

DEDICATION

This special book is lovingly dedicated to all the amazing children out there - the dreamers, the thinkers, the explorers, and the creators. Yes, you! The one holding this book in your hands, embarking on a new journey of self-discovery and growth.

You may be small, but we know your heart is mighty and your spirit is strong. Your curiosity lights up the world, and your laughter is the sweetest melody. You are full of boundless potential, waiting to blossom. This book is a little tool to help you navigate through the waves of emotions and challenges, to find your calm and build your strength.

To the parents, teachers, and caregivers who guide these wonderful children, this book is also for you. Thank you for your patience, your love, and your tireless dedication. Your work is the garden in which our children grow.

And lastly, this book is dedicated to every person who believes in the power of young minds. Let this be a reminder that every child is capable of incredible things. As they learn and grow, so does our hope for a brighter future.

Remember, no matter where you are or how you feel, you are never alone in your journey. We believe in you, and we're cheering you on every step of the way. So let's begin this adventure together. You're going to be great.

Enjoy the journey, dear readers. This one's for you.

TABLE OF CONTENT

GUIDE ON UTILIZING THIS WORKBOOK ON AN EBOOK DEVICE

If you are using this workbook on a touch-screen device, you have the ability to add notes and highlight text, just as you would in a physical workbook.

Certain sections will prompt you to write answers or personal responses. It's straightforward – give it a try right here: _____.

Using your finger, tap and hold for a few moments on the line above. Depending on the device you are using, an icon, such as a magnifying glass, will appear. Lift your finger, and an options menu will show up. Select "Note" (or "Notes") to add and save your own text. Once you're done, an icon or highlighted area will remain, which you can always return to and tap if you want to reopen, read, or edit your note.

The same tap-and-hold options menu offers "Highlight" or "Color," which you can select if you want to highlight a passage or "check" a box. Experiment with it: by swiping your finger before releasing, you can select entire sentences or paragraphs. The options menu also offers "Bookmark" for when you want quick access back to certain pages.

This method is the same on nearly all touch-screen eBook devices, but there may be slight variations. If you'd like more information specific to the device you're holding in your hands, a quick online search will yield the best results.

DEAR PARENT

If you've picked up this book, chances are, you are a parent, relative, educator, therapist, or even a patient who is seeking to understand more about Dialectical Behavior Therapy, often referred to as DBT. You deserve a pat on the back for your proactive approach towards mental health. By making this choice, you're playing a key role in fostering the well-being of yourself or a loved one.

My name is Payton Black, and I am a licensed child psychologist. I work with people who are leveraging DBT, as well as their caregivers. I myself have had close family members who have benefited immensely from this therapeutic approach. The ups and downs of mental health have been a constant companion in my life. I have shared the joys of triumphs and wept during the tough times. I have witnessed the beautiful transformation that comes from successful DBT.

I've often asked myself, why can't they just snap out of it like those who seem so mentally stable? Over time, though, I've grown to appreciate and respect the unique perspectives and resilience that people undergoing DBT have. They possess an extraordinary depth of understanding and empathy, and their courage is second to none. Their unique way of confronting and handling their mental health has been a profound learning experience for me.

In this book, my goal is to help you or your loved one understand that mental health difficulties aren't a defect, but a part of their unique human experience. With the right skills and mindset, these challenges can become sources of strength and growth. I employ a "strength-based approach," focusing on the inherent strengths within each individual, to cultivate self-confidence and resilience. It's about highlighting what they can do right, rather than what they're doing wrong.

Time is of the essence, and I understand that frustration tolerance can be low, both in caregivers and those undergoing therapy. So, I have strived to present easy-to-follow exercises and activities that can be performed independently. I have used minimal equipment and varied the activities to suit different personalities and preferences. These activities have been tested and proved effective with my family members and patients.

Some readers may use this book independently, while others may prefer a team approach, engaging in activities together with their support systems. Different activities may seem easier or more challenging based on personal experience and comfort levels. That's perfectly fine! The important thing is to feel empowered and in control while engaging in these activities.

At times, some may need help or support to complete a given task, and that's completely okay. You may find them meditating in the middle of the living room or sticking affirmations on the refrigerator. They may also request your help to set goals and rewards for their progress. Whether they choose to engage in these activities alone or with others, it's all a part of the journey.

Please remember: This book is intended to be a complementary tool to a comprehensive DBT program. Always work closely with your mental health professionals to ensure the best possible outcome. Let's embark on this journey towards mental wellness together!

DEAR KID

HIYA! WELCOME ON BOARD! I'M DR. PAYTON, a psychologistt with extensive experience in helping individuals with emotional regulation challenges. I genuinely believe that everyone should navigate life's waves with confidence and serenity, so I've put together this guide filled with exercises, mindfulness practices, and handy tips to guide you in this journey of self-discovery and emotional mastery.

First off, let's explore what DBT is. You may have stumbled upon this term before, and you're curious to understand its real essence. DBT stands for Dialectical Behavior Therapy. Now, that's a mouthful, right? My ten-year-old daughter, Alice, who's very observant and loves to understand what mommy does, summarizes it as "a way to help people handle their feelings better." And she's right on the money! DBT is a therapy approach that provides skills for managing painful emotions and decreasing conflict in relationships. It could be particularly helpful if you've found yourself overwhelmed by emotions, or if you're struggling to maintain stable and fulfilling relationships.

Think about a person who needs a life jacket while swimming. They can swim but might get exhausted quickly or might panic if they go out of their depth. With a life jacket, they can float, feel safer, and enjoy the water. Just like the life jacket, my aim is to provide you with tools, strategies, and fun exercises—the support—you need to understand and manage your emotions and relationships better.

Emotional challenges or mental health issues are not your fault, nor are they something you brought upon yourself. They also have nothing to do with your upbringing or your diet. You are who you are, and you are fantastic!

Also, remember that you're not alone. Millions of people around the world are on this journey too. Many successful individuals have benefited from DBT. Famous personalities like Lady Gaga and Demi Lovato have openly spoken about their mental health struggles and the benefits they've gained from therapy like DBT.

Brandon Marshall, an NFL player, is an advocate for DBT after it helped him with his borderline personality disorder.

There are countless CEOs, teachers, doctors, firefighters, engineers, artists, journalists, therapists, and even some of our most beloved authors who have used DBT skills. Some say the brilliant philosopher, Socrates, utilized dialectics, a principle central to DBT. You can still live a successful, fulfilling life, just like anyone else. And I'm here to help!

Together, we will learn new skills and practices that are not only helpful but also engaging. You might not even realize you're learning! But as you apply these skills, you'll find that you are better equipped to navigate the stormy seas of emotions. If you read and apply the suggestions in this guide, you will feel more at peace and understand more about yourself and how to manage your emotions and relationships. Are you excited to begin this journey? Let's dive in!

CHAPTER 1: INTRODUCTION TO DBT FOR KIDS

"Through the lens of DBT, we don't merely survive our storms, we learn to dance in the rain, transforming our emotions into graceful steps towards a more balanced and peaceful life."

What is DBT?

Have you ever heard of something called DBT? It might sound like a secret code or a new video game, but it's actually something even cooler. DBT stands for Dialectical Behavior Therapy. That's a mouthful, isn't it? Don't worry, though! We're going to break it down together, and it's going to be fun and interesting!

First off, let's talk about the word "Dialectical". This big word means finding the balance between two things that seem to be opposite. Imagine trying to stand on one leg. It's all about finding the right balance so you don't fall over, right? Well, in life, we also need to find the right balance between accepting things as they are and working to make things better. That's what "Dialectical" is all about!

Next up is "Behavior". That's a simpler one, right? Behavior is just anything we do. It can be how we talk, how we act, how we react to things, and even how we think. So, when we talk about "Behavior" in DBT, we mean all the things we do, say, and think.

Finally, "Therapy". When you think of therapy, you might think of going to a doctor when you're sick. But therapy can also mean learning new skills and strategies to deal with problems. It's like going to a coach who helps you improve your soccer skills, but in this case, we're improving our emotion-handling skills.

So, when we put it all together, DBT is like a special coaching class where we learn to balance our feelings, actions, and thoughts. It helps us understand our emotions better, and shows us how to react when things get tough or when we're upset.

Let's say you're really, really upset because your best friend didn't invite you to their birthday party. That hurts, doesn't it? DBT helps us handle situations like these. It doesn't magically make the pain go away, but it does teach us how to cope with it in a healthy way. It might teach us to take deep breaths, think about the situation calmly, and talk to our friend about how we're feeling.

And guess what? DBT isn't just for tough times. It can also make the good times even better! It teaches us to be present and enjoy the moment, like really tasting that ice cream on a hot summer day, or feeling the grass under our feet in the park.

In a nutshell, DBT is a toolbox filled with strategies that can help us in our lives. It's about finding balance, understanding ourselves better, and dealing with the ups and downs of life in a healthier way. And the best part? Anyone can learn DBT skills, even awesome kids like you! So, are you ready to explore this amazing toolbox with me? Let's dive in!

YOU'RE THE CAPTAIN OF YOUR EMOTION-SHIP

You're stronger than you think! With Dialectical Behavior Therapy (DBT), you're learning to become the captain of your own "Emotion-Ship". Just like a captain sails through stormy seas, you can navigate through tough emotions. Remember, it's okay to feel all kinds of feelings. And it's super cool that you're learning how to handle them in a healthy way. Keep practicing your DBT skills, because every day, you're becoming more awesome at understanding yourself and others. You're doing a fantastic job, and we're so proud of you. So keep sailing, brave captain, and remember: You've got this!

Activity: Draw Your Own DBT Poster

Objective: The goal of this activity is to help you understand the key components of DBT by creating a colorful and fun poster. This poster can be a great reminder of what you're learning and a way to share DBT skills with others.

Materials:

- A large piece of poster paper

- Colored markers, pencils, or crayons

- Stickers or other decorations (optional)

Instructions:

1. **Create a Title:** At the top of your poster, write a title like "My DBT Skills" or "DBT Superpowers". Make it big and bold!

2. **Divide Your Poster:** Split your poster into four sections, one for each of the main DBT skills: Mindfulness, Distress Tolerance, Emotion Regulation, and Interpersonal Effectiveness.

3. **Mindfulness:** In the Mindfulness section, draw a picture that helps you remember to be present and aware. You might draw a picture of someone meditating, a brain, or an eye to represent focus.

4. **Distress Tolerance:** In the Distress Tolerance section, illustrate how you can cope with tough emotions or situations. You could draw a heart to represent self-love, a shield to represent protection, or a wave to represent riding out tough times.

5. **Emotion Regulation:** In the Emotion Regulation section, create an image that reminds you of managing your emotions. You might draw a thermometer for measuring feelings, a sunny and stormy sky to show all types of feelings, or a rollercoaster to represent the ups and downs of emotions.

6. **Interpersonal Effectiveness:** In the Interpersonal Effectiveness section, depict ways to interact well with others. You could draw two people shaking hands, a speech bubble for effective communication, or a heart to show kindness.

7. **Decorate Your Poster:** Now comes the fun part! Decorate your poster with colors, patterns, stickers, or whatever you like. Make it your own!

8. **Hang Your Poster:** Once you're done, find a good place to hang your poster. It could be in your room, on the refrigerator, or anywhere else you'll see it often. This way, you'll have a constant reminder of your DBT skills.

Remember, there's no right or wrong way to do this activity. It's all about expressing yourself and understanding DBT in your own way. So let your creativity fly!

Exercise: Multiple Choice Questions on DBT

1. What does DBT stand for?

   - A) Direct Behavior Training

   - B) Dialectical Behavior Therapy

   - C) Direct Behavior Therapy

   - D) Dialectical Behavior Training

2. What does the 'Dialectical' in DBT mean?

   - A) Learning to speak in a new language

   - B) Finding the balance between two opposite things

   - C) Learning to behave better

   - D) Understanding your feelings

3. Which of the following is NOT a skill taught in DBT?

   - A) Mindfulness

   - B) Distress Tolerance

   - C) Emotion Regulation

   - D) Math Calculation

4. How can DBT help us in daily life?

   - A) By teaching us how to ride a bike

   - B) By helping us understand and handle our feelings better

   - C) By helping us learn a new instrument

   - D) By teaching us how to cook

5. Mindfulness, a key part of DBT, teaches us to:

   - A) Always be thinking about the past or future

- B) Be present and aware of the moment

- C) Ignore our feelings

- D) Always be talking to others

Remember, these questions are just a starting point. Feel free to modify them or add more questions to fit the lessons you've covered in your workbook.

Why is DBT Helpful?

So, why is DBT helpful? Well, imagine you're learning to ride a bicycle. At first, it's a bit tricky. You might fall off a few times, or maybe you can't steer straight. But then, someone teaches you how to balance, how to pedal smoothly, and how to turn without tipping over. Suddenly, biking becomes a lot easier, right?

DBT is like that, but for our feelings and thoughts. Sometimes, we all feel a bit like we're trying to ride a bike for the first time. Our emotions can feel too big and wobbly, our thoughts can go in directions we didn't expect, and we might react to things in ways that don't make us feel good afterwards.

DBT is like a friendly bike teacher for our minds. It helps us understand our feelings and thoughts better. It teaches us how to balance them, how to steer them in the right direction, and how not to fall over when things get a bit tricky.

For example, let's say you're feeling really, really angry because your little brother just broke your favorite toy. That's a big, strong emotion, isn't it? DBT can help you understand why you're feeling so angry, and it can give you skills to calm down and talk to your brother about it instead of shouting or getting into a fight.

DBT can also help us with our relationships – that's just a fancy word for how we get along with other people. Maybe you're having trouble making friends at school, or you're not sure how to stand up to a bully. DBT gives us skills for these situations too!

It's not just for the tough times, though. DBT can also make the good times even better. It teaches us mindfulness, which is a special way of paying attention that can help us enjoy our favorite activities, like playing a game or eating ice cream, even more.

So, DBT is a set of tools for your mind, like a superhero utility belt for your brain. It helps us handle big feelings, think clearly, make good choices, and get along better with others. And just like riding a bike, the more we practice DBT, the better we get at it.

Now, isn't that helpful?

Remember, it's okay to ask for help and to talk about your feelings. Everyone needs a little help sometimes, and DBT is a way for us to get that help. So, let's start our exciting journey with DBT together!

Activity: Create Your DBT Benefit List

Materials Needed:

- A sheet of paper (you can use any color you like!)

- Markers, colored pencils, or crayons

- Stickers or glitter (if you want to make your list extra fun and sparkly)

Instructions:

1. **Think about what you learned:** Before we start, take a moment to think about what you've learned so far about DBT. Remember, it's like a superhero utility belt for your brain, helping you understand and manage your feelings, think clearly, make good decisions, and get along with others.

2. **Write a title:** At the top of your paper, write "My DBT Benefit List". Make it bold and colorful!

3. **List the benefits:** Now, it's time to make your list. Think about the benefits of DBT and write them down. Here are some ideas to get you started:

   - Helps me understand my feelings better

   - Teaches me how to calm down when I'm upset

   - Gives me skills to solve problems

   - Helps me make friends and get along with others

   - Helps me enjoy good times even more through mindfulness

   - Helps me stand up for myself

Remember, these are just ideas. You can write down any benefits you think DBT has!

4. **Draw or decorate:** Once you've written down all the benefits, it's time to make your list look amazing. You can draw little pictures next to each benefit,

or decorate your list with stickers or glitter. Make it as colorful and creative as you want!

5. **Share your list:** If you're comfortable, share your list with someone you trust, like a parent, teacher, or friend. They might be interested to learn about DBT and how it's helping you.

6. **Keep your list:** Keep your list somewhere safe. You can look at it whenever you're practicing your DBT skills, or anytime you want to remind yourself of all the great ways DBT is helping you.

Remember, there's no right or wrong way to do this activity. The most important thing is to think about how DBT can help you and to have fun creating your list!

Exercise: Matching Benefits with Real-life Situations

Materials Needed:

- The DBT Benefit List you created in the previous activity

- A sheet of paper

- A pen or pencil

Instructions:

1. **Review your DBT Benefit List:** Take a look at your DBT Benefit List that you created in the previous activity. Refresh your memory on the benefits you listed.

2. **Prepare your paper:** On your new sheet of paper, draw two columns. Label the left column "DBT Benefits" and the right column "Real-Life Situations".

3. **List the benefits:** In the left column, list down all the benefits from your DBT Benefit List.

4. **Think of real-life situations:** Now for the right column, think of a real-life situation where each DBT benefit could be helpful. Write down these situations next to the matching benefit. For example, if one of your benefits is "Helps me calm down when I'm upset", you might write "When my little sister takes my toys without asking" in the Real-Life Situations column.

5. **Discuss your answers:** If possible, review your answers with a parent, teacher, or friend. They might have additional insights or suggestions for other situations where you can apply DBT benefits.

Here's an example of how your list might look:

DBT Benefits	Real-Life Situations
Helps me understand my feelings better	When I feel sad after losing a game
Teaches me how to calm down when I'm upset	When my little sister takes my toys without asking
Gives me skills to solve problems	When I have a disagreement with my friend
Helps me make friends and get along with others	When I meet new kids at summer camp
Helps me enjoy good times even more through mindfulness	When I'm eating my favorite ice cream
Helps me stand up for myself	When someone at school is being mean to me

This exercise should help you understand how DBT can be applied in real-life situations. Remember, it's okay to ask for help if you're having trouble, and it's great to keep practicing your DBT skills!

CHAPTER 2: UNDERSTANDING EMOTIONS

Types of Emotions

Just like animals in the wild, emotions come in many different shapes and sizes. Some emotions are big and loud, like a roaring lion, while others are small and quiet, like a chirping bird. Let's take a closer look at some of the most common types of emotions that we all feel.

- **Happiness** is a joyful emotion that you might feel when you're having fun, playing with your friends, or eating your favorite ice cream. It's like a bouncy kangaroo, jumping around and making you feel light and full of energy.

- **Sadness** is a quiet emotion that might sneak up on you like a gentle turtle when something doesn't go the way you wanted, or when you miss someone. Even though it might make you feel a bit slow or heavy, remember that it's okay to feel sad sometimes. It's a part of life, and it helps us appreciate the happy times more.

- **Fear** can feel like a big, scary elephant in the room. It shows up when we're worried about something that might happen, like before a big test at school or trying something new. It's important to remember that everyone feels afraid sometimes, and it's okay to talk about it. After all, even elephants are afraid of tiny mice!

- **Anger** can be like a roaring lion, loud and hard to ignore. We might feel angry when someone breaks our toy, takes our turn, or when things just don't seem fair. While it's okay to feel angry, it's important to remember not to let the lion out of its cage—we should express our anger in ways that don't hurt others or ourselves.

- **Surprise** can pop up like a playful monkey, making us jump with excitement or shock. This emotion comes when something unexpected happens, like getting a surprise gift or being startled by a loud noise.

- **Disgust** can creep up like a slithering snake when we encounter something we really don't like. Maybe it's the taste of a food we don't like, or a bad smell. It's our body's way of telling us that something might not be good for us.

Just like in a jungle, sometimes different emotions can appear at the same time or one after the other, and that's perfectly normal. Maybe you've felt happy and sad at the same time, or felt scared but also a little excited. Emotions can be confusing sometimes, but they are all part of our journey.

Remember, there's no such thing as a "bad" emotion—every emotion has a purpose and helps us understand ourselves and the world around us better. So, the next time you're feeling a strong emotion, take a moment to understand what it might be telling you. Maybe it's a roaring lion of anger, or a bouncy kangaroo of joy. Whatever it is, remember that it's okay to feel your feelings, and that you're not alone in your emotional jungle.

Activity: Emotion Sorting Game

In this activity, we are going to become explorers, but instead of exploring a jungle, we are going to explore our emotions!

Materials Needed:

- Emotion Cards (You can make these at home! On small pieces of paper, write the names of different emotions like Happy, Sad, Angry, Excited, Scared, Surprised, Disgusted, and so on.)

- Three boxes or baskets labeled "Feels Good," "Feels Uncomfortable," and "Mixed Feelings"

Steps:

1. **Prepare Your Emotion Cards:** With the help of an adult, write down different emotion words on small pieces of paper. These are your Emotion Cards. Make sure to include a wide range of emotions!

2. **Set up Your Boxes or Baskets:** Take three boxes or baskets and label them as "Feels Good," "Feels Uncomfortable," and "Mixed Feelings."

3. **Sort the Emotions:** Pick one Emotion Card at a time. Think about how this emotion makes you feel. If it's an emotion that makes you feel good, like happiness or excitement, place it in the "Feels Good" box. If it's an emotion that makes you feel uncomfortable, like sadness or anger, place it in the "Feels Uncomfortable" box. If it's an emotion that can make you feel both good and uncomfortable at the same time, like surprise, place it in the "Mixed Feelings" box.

4. **Discussion:** Once you have sorted all the emotions, take some time to discuss your choices with an adult. Why did you place certain emotions in certain boxes? Were there any emotions that were difficult to place? This is a great time to talk about how it's okay to feel all kinds of emotions.

Exercise: Identify the Emotion Worksheet

This worksheet consists of several scenarios. Each scenario is followed by three options representing different emotions. Your task is to read each scenario and identify the most likely emotion that the person in the scenario is experiencing.

Materials Needed:

- Pencil or pen
- Printed "Identify the Emotion" worksheet

Worksheet Content:

1. **Scenario:** Emily's best friend just gave her a surprise birthday gift.
   - A) Angry
   - B) Surprised
   - C) Disgusted

2. **Scenario:** Oliver's ice cream fell on the ground just as he was about to take the first bite.
   - A) Excited
   - B) Sad
   - C) Happy

3. **Scenario:** Mia saw a spider in her room.
   - A) Scared
   - B) Angry
   - C) Excited

4. **Scenario:** Liam won the first prize in a drawing competition.
   - A) Happy
   - B) Scared
   - C) Disgusted

5. **Scenario:** Sofia's little brother broke her favorite toy.
   - A) Happy
   - B) Angry
   - C) Surprised

6. **Scenario:** Noah did not do well on his math test.

- A) Excited
- B) Disgusted
- C) Sad

Instructions:

Read each scenario and think about how the person in the scenario might be feeling. Circle the emotion that you think best fits each situation.

Remember, this is not about right or wrong answers. This exercise is to help you think about different situations and the emotions they might bring up. Once you're done, you can discuss your answers with an adult and talk about why you chose the emotions you did.

This exercise is designed to help children develop empathy and understanding of emotions by putting themselves in the shoes of others and identifying what they might be feeling in different situations.

How We Experience Emotions

Let's take a fun journey into the world of our feelings! You know, those things that make you happy when you're playing with your best friend, or sad when you lose your favorite toy? Those are called emotions, and they are an important part of our lives.

Imagine emotions as different colors of paint. Just as a beautiful painting has a lot of different colors, our lives are filled with a mix of different emotions. Sometimes, you might feel one strong emotion, like when you're really, really happy on your birthday. That's like a bright splash of yellow on a painting. Other times, you might feel a blend of emotions, like feeling excited and nervous before a big soccer game. That's like mixing blue and red paint to make purple.

But how do we experience these emotions? Let's find out!

The first thing to remember is that everyone experiences emotions differently, and that's okay. Just like how some people love the taste of broccoli while others don't, we all have different feelings about different things.

Our emotions usually start with something happening around us. This could be something big, like moving to a new city, or something small, like seeing a cute puppy in the park. These are called "triggers". They're like the brush that starts to spread color on our painting.

Once a trigger happens, our brain starts to react. It's like a super-fast computer that processes what's happening and decides how we should feel about it. Sometimes, this happens so quickly that we don't even realize it!

Next, our body joins in. Have you noticed how your heart beats faster when you're scared, or how you start to smile when you're happy? That's your body showing your emotions. It's like adding more details to our painting, making it more vibrant and full of life.

And finally, we react based on how we're feeling. If we're feeling angry, we might yell or stomp our feet. If we're feeling excited, we might jump around or cheer. And if we're feeling sad, we might cry or want to be alone for a while.

Just like how every painting is unique, every person's emotions are unique too. Even though we might all feel the same basic emotions—like happiness, sadness, anger, fear, and love—the way we experience them can be very different.

Remember, it's perfectly normal to have all kinds of feelings, and it's important to talk about them. So next time you feel a strong emotion, try to notice what triggered it, how your brain and body reacted, and how you responded. That's the beautiful, colorful painting of your emotions!

Activity: Emotion Body Map Art Project

Objective: This activity helps children understand how different emotions can be felt in different parts of the body. It's a fun and creative way to explore emotions and their physical impact.

Materials needed:

1. Large sheet of paper

2. Colored pencils or markers

3. Stickers (optional)

Instructions:

1. *Draw your body:* Lay the large sheet of paper on the floor. You can either draw around your body, trace your shadow, or simply draw a large outline of a person.

2. *Think about different emotions:* Now, think about different emotions you experience, like happiness, sadness, anger, excitement, or fear. You can use a list of emotions to help you if you want.

3. *Decide on colors for each emotion:* Pick a different color for each emotion. For example, you might choose yellow for happiness, blue for sadness, red for anger, and so on. Write down which color represents which emotion.

4. *Map your emotions:* Now, close your eyes and think about where you feel these emotions in your body. For example, do you feel a fluttering in your stomach when you're excited? Or a tightness in your chest when you're scared? Do your hands clench when you're angry? Take the colored pencils or markers and color in the parts of the body where you feel each emotion.

5. *Decorate:* After you have filled in your body map, use the stickers to decorate it. You can also use your markers or colored pencils to add more details or designs.

6. *Share and discuss:* If you're comfortable, you can share your emotion body map with others and talk about it. What did you notice? Was there anything that surprised you? Remember, there's no right or wrong way to do this. Everyone's emotion body map will look different because we all experience emotions in our own unique way.

Wrap-up: This activity helps children understand how emotions aren't just something we feel in our minds, but also in our bodies. It can be a powerful tool for helping them understand and manage their emotions better.

Exercise: Emotion Journaling

Objective: The goal of this exercise is to encourage children to express their feelings and understand their emotional reactions to different events in their lives. Journaling can also help them identify patterns in their emotional responses over time.

Materials needed:

1. A journal or notebook

2. Pen or pencil

3. Colored pencils or markers (optional)

Instructions:

1. *Create a journal:* First, you need a journal. This could be a simple notebook, or you can create your own by stapling together some pieces of paper. You might want to decorate the cover to make it personal and special.

2. *Write daily:* Try to write in your journal every day. You can write about something that happened that day, how you felt about it, and why you think you felt that way. You could write about a conversation you had, a movie you watched, a game you played, or even a dream you had.

3. *Include details:* When you write about an event, try to include as many details as possible. What happened? Who was there? What did you see, hear, or smell? How did it make you feel?

4. *Color your emotions:* If you want, you can use different colors to represent different emotions. For example, you might use yellow for happy entries, blue for sad entries, and red for angry entries. This can make your journal more colorful and help you visualize your emotions.

5. *Reflect:* After you've been writing for a while, look back at your previous entries. Do you notice any patterns? Are there certain things that consistently make you happy, sad, or angry? How have your emotions changed over time?

Wrap-up: Emotion journaling is a powerful tool for understanding your feelings and how they influence your life. It's a safe space where you can express yourself freely. And remember, your journal is for you, so there's no right or wrong way to do it. The most important thing is to be honest with yourself and your feelings.

CHAPTER 3: MINDFULNESS

Understanding Mindfulness

Have you ever sat down and enjoyed a piece of candy, savoring each tiny bit of its taste? Or maybe you've been so engrossed in a good book or game that you lost track of time? If you've had experiences like these, then you already know a little bit about mindfulness!

Mindfulness is like using a special magnifying glass for your life. It's all about focusing on the 'now' and paying attention to what's happening around you and inside you. Imagine you're a detective, and your job is to notice all the little details of your life, like the taste of your breakfast, the sound of birds chirping, or how your breath feels going in and out of your nose.

When you practice mindfulness, you don't worry about yesterday or tomorrow. You're just paying attention to what is happening right now. It's like pausing a movie to notice all the details in a scene.

Let's try a fun example. Take a moment to look at your hand. Really look at it as if it's the first time you've ever seen a hand. Notice the lines on your palm, how your fingers move, and even how your skin feels. Congratulations! You've just practiced mindfulness.

Why is mindfulness important? Well, think about a time when you were upset or worried. Maybe you had a test coming up, or maybe you were upset about a fight with a friend. During those times, it's easy for our minds to get stuck in what we call 'worry loops'. But when you practice mindfulness, you can help your mind get unstuck from these loops.

Mindfulness helps us to calm down and to deal with stress better. It can help us focus, and it can even make us feel happier. It's like a superpower for your brain!

So how can you practice mindfulness? There are lots of ways! You can take deep breaths and pay attention to how they feel. You can eat a snack and take the time to really taste it. You can go for a walk and listen to all the sounds around you. The key is to slow down and pay attention to the moment.

Remember, mindfulness is not about clearing your mind or stopping your thoughts. That's a big myth. It's all about noticing your thoughts and feelings without judgment. Imagine your thoughts are like clouds in the sky. Sometimes they're fluffy and light, and sometimes they're dark and stormy. But no matter what, they're always changing, and they don't define who you are.

So, give mindfulness a try! It might feel strange at first, but that's okay. Like anything new, it takes practice. But once you get the hang of it, you might just find that you're more calm, focused, and happy in your day-to-day life.

And always remember, every moment is a new chance to be mindful!

Activity: Mindful Breathing Exercise

Objective: To help kids practice mindfulness and become more aware of their breathing.

Materials Needed: None

Instructions:

1. **Find a quiet place:** Start by finding a quiet place where you can sit comfortably. You can sit on a chair, on the floor, or even on a soft carpet. Make sure you're feeling comfortable and relaxed.

2. **Sit up straight:** Now, sit up straight. Pretend there's a string attached to the top of your head that's pulling you gently up towards the sky. But make sure your body is relaxed, not stiff.

3. **Close your eyes:** If it feels okay, gently close your eyes. If you'd rather keep them open, that's fine too. Just find a spot in front of you to rest your gaze.

4. **Focus on your breath:** Now, it's time to pay attention to your breathing. Notice how the air feels as it goes in and out of your nose. Is it warm? Is it cool? Don't try to change your breathing, just notice it.

5. **Count your breaths:** As you breathe in, silently count "one" in your mind. As you breathe out, count "two". Keep going until you reach "ten", and then start back at "one". If you lose track, that's okay! Just start again at "one".

6. **Notice your thoughts:** It's natural for thoughts to pop up while you're trying to focus on your breath. That's okay! Imagine that your thoughts are like bubbles. When one pops up, just notice it, and then let it pop and disappear. Then, gently bring your attention back to your breath.

7. **Keep going:** Try to keep this going for a few minutes. It might seem like a long time, but with practice, it will become easier.

Reflection: After you're done, take a moment to notice how you feel. Do you feel calmer? More focused? Remember, there's no right or wrong way to feel. The important thing is to notice how you feel and accept it without judgment.

Remember, practicing mindfulness is like training a puppy. Sometimes your mind will wander off, just like a puppy might run off to explore. But just like you'd gently bring a puppy back, you can gently bring your mind back to your breath.

So, keep practicing this Mindful Breathing Exercise. With time, you'll find it easier to focus, feel calmer, and handle stress better. Just like any other skill, the more you practice, the better you'll get!

Exercise: Mindful Moments Journal

Objective: The goal of this exercise is to help kids practice mindfulness in their daily lives and reflect on their experiences.

Materials Needed: A notebook or journal, a pen or pencil

Instructions:

1. **Set up your journal:** Find a notebook or journal that you can use for this exercise. It can be any notebook you like. At the top of a new page, write "My Mindful Moments Journal".

2. **Choose your mindful moment:** Each day, choose a moment to practice mindfulness. It could be while you're eating breakfast, during recess at school, or while brushing your teeth. The key is to choose a moment where you can slow down and pay close attention to your experiences.

3. **Practice mindfulness:** During your chosen moment, slow down and start noticing what's happening. What can you see, hear, smell, taste, or touch? What thoughts are passing through your mind? What emotions are you feeling? Remember, mindfulness is all about noticing these things without judgment.

4. **Write about your experience:** After your mindful moment, write about your experience in your journal. Here are some questions you can answer:

   - What did you notice during your mindful moment?

   - What thoughts came into your mind?

   - How did you feel before, during, and after the moment?

   - Did anything surprise you about this experience?

5. **Reflect on your entries:** Once a week, take some time to read through your journal entries and reflect on them. Do you notice any patterns? Are there

certain things that often distract you? How does practicing mindfulness affect your mood?

Tips:

- Remember, there's no right or wrong way to practice mindfulness. It's all about noticing and accepting your experiences.

- If you find it hard to remember to do your mindful moment, you can set a reminder on a phone or clock, or ask someone to remind you.

- If writing isn't your thing, you can also draw or doodle about your mindful moments.

Practicing mindfulness and keeping a Mindful Moments Journal can help you become more aware of your thoughts and feelings. It can help you feel calmer, happier, and more focused. So, give it a try and see what you discover!

Applying Mindfulness to Daily Life

Have you ever eaten a snack while watching TV and suddenly realized your snack is all gone? You didn't even notice you were eating it because your attention was on the show. This is an example of not being mindful. So, what does it mean to be mindful?

Imagine you're a superhero, and your superpower is to slow down time. You notice everything around you. You see the colors and shapes of things more brightly. You hear sounds that you usually don't pay attention to. You feel more deeply. You're not thinking about yesterday or tomorrow. You're right here, right now. That's mindfulness!

Mindfulness is like turning on your superhero power. It's about being fully present and paying attention to this very moment. It's about noticing your thoughts, feelings, and everything that's happening around you without judging it as good or bad.

So, how can you use this superpower in your daily life? Let's find out.

1. **Mindful Breathing:** One way to be mindful is by focusing on your breath. You can do this anytime and anywhere. Just close your eyes and notice how the air feels going in and out of your nose. Is it cool or warm? Fast or slow? It's like a game of noticing!

2. **Mindful Eating:** Remember the TV and snack example? Try eating your snack without doing anything else. Notice its taste, texture, and smell. You might find that your snack tastes even better when you eat mindfully!

3. **Mindful Listening:** The next time you're outside, close your eyes and listen. What do you hear? Birds chirping? Cars passing by? Wind rustling the leaves? By doing this, you're practicing mindfulness.

4. **Mindful Moving:** When you're walking or playing, pay attention to how your body feels. Notice how your legs move when you run, how your arms swing, or how your feet touch the ground.

5. **Mindful Feelings:** It's important to notice your feelings too. If you're feeling happy, sad, excited, or upset, just notice it. Say to yourself, "I notice I'm feeling..." and say the emotion. It's okay to feel all types of feelings. Remember, superheroes don't judge!

6. **Mindful Thoughts:** Sometimes, our minds are full of thoughts, like a busy bee hive. It's normal! But instead of getting lost in those thoughts, try to observe them as if they're clouds passing in the sky.

By practicing mindfulness every day, you can become a Mindfulness Superhero! You'll find that you enjoy your daily activities more, understand your feelings better, and even handle tough times more easily. So, ready to turn on your superpower? Let's get started with mindfulness today!

Activity: Mindful Eating Experience

Materials:

1. A small piece of fruit (like a grape, a slice of apple, or a strawberry)

2. A quiet space

Instructions:

1. **Look:** Take the piece of fruit and really look at it. Notice its colors, shapes, and sizes. Does it have any spots or bumps? Is it shiny or dull?

2. **Touch:** Close your eyes and touch the fruit. What does it feel like? Is it smooth, bumpy, sticky, or squishy?

3. **Smell:** Now, smell the fruit. Does it have a strong smell or a light one? Does it smell sweet, sour, or something else?

4. **Listen:** Hold the fruit close to your ear and squeeze it gently. Does it make a sound?

5. **Taste:** Now, take a small bite but don't chew yet. Keep it on your tongue. How does it taste? Is it sweet, sour, or a mix of both?

6. **Chew:** Start chewing slowly and notice how the taste changes. Pay attention to the sounds it makes in your mouth.

7. **Swallow:** When you're ready, swallow the fruit. Can you feel it going down your throat and into your stomach?

Congratulations! You just did a mindful eating exercise. How was it different from the way you usually eat? Did you notice anything new about the fruit that you never noticed before?

This activity can be a fun way for kids to slow down and pay attention to the experience of eating. It's a great introduction to the practice of mindfulness, and can be repeated with different foods for a variety of experiences.

Exercise: Mindfulness Scavenger Hunt

Materials:

1. Mindfulness Scavenger Hunt checklist (see below)
2. A pen or pencil

Mindfulness Scavenger Hunt Checklist:

- Find something that...
    - You can touch that feels soft
    - You can touch that feels rough
    - Smells sweet
    - Smells earthy
    - You can taste (make sure it's edible and safe!)
    - Makes a quiet sound
    - Makes a loud sound
    - Is the brightest color you can find
    - Is the coolest color you can find
    - Makes you feel happy when you see it
    - You think is beautiful
    - You've never noticed before

Instructions:

1. Take your checklist and go to a safe outdoor or indoor space where you can explore.
2. Look at the first item on your checklist. Spend some time exploring until you find something that matches the description.
3. When you find something, take a moment to really look at it, touch it, smell it, or listen to it. Pay attention to all the details.
4. Once you've fully experienced it, you can check it off your list.
5. Move on to the next item and repeat the process.

6. Remember, this is not a race. Take your time to really engage with each item you find.

7. Once you've found everything, sit down and think about the experience. What did you notice? Did anything surprise you?

The Mindfulness Scavenger Hunt not only helps kids practice mindfulness, but also encourages them to interact with and appreciate their surroundings in new ways.

CHAPTER 4: DISTRESS TOLERANCE

Understanding Distress Tolerance

Imagine you're playing a video game. You're so close to winning, but suddenly, you lose! That feeling you get, that disappointment or frustration, that's called distress. Sometimes, life is like that video game. Things don't always go as we hope or plan, and it can make us feel upset or uncomfortable. These feelings are perfectly normal, but the key is learning how to deal with them, and that's where distress tolerance comes in.

So, what is distress tolerance? It's like having a superpower that helps you handle tough feelings without letting them take over. Think of it as having a mental superhero shield that can block those upsetting emotions, allowing you to react in a calm and controlled way. Isn't that awesome?

Imagine if that video game had a special button that could help you calm down and try again without getting too upset. That's exactly what distress tolerance skills can do for you in real life. They can help you to navigate difficult moments more smoothly, so you can bounce back quicker when things don't go your way.

Now, you might be wondering, "How do I get this superpower?" Well, the good news is, anyone can learn distress tolerance! It's all about practicing different techniques that help you calm down when you're upset. One such technique is distraction. For instance, if you're upset about losing the game, maybe you could play with your pet, draw a picture, or listen to your favorite song. These activities can help shift your focus away from the distressing event and towards something more enjoyable.

Another technique is self-soothing. This could be anything that helps you feel calm and relaxed. Maybe it's taking slow, deep breaths, or it might be imagining a safe, happy place in your mind. It's like giving your mind a warm, cozy blanket to help it feel better.

Finally, remember that it's okay to feel upset sometimes. It's a part of life, and everyone goes through it. What's important is how you handle those feelings. With distress tolerance, you can become like a superhero, able to face any challenge with courage and calmness. So, next time you face a difficult situation, remember your mental superhero shield and use your distress tolerance skills. You've got this!

Activity: Distress Tolerance Role-Play

Objective: This activity aims to help kids practice distress tolerance skills in a fun and interactive way through role-play.

Materials Needed: Scenario cards (prepared in advance), a safe and comfortable space to act out the scenarios.

Instructions:

1. **Preparation:** Before the activity, create several scenario cards. Each card should describe a situation that could cause distress. For instance, one card might say, "You studied hard for a test, but you didn't get the grade you wanted." Another might say, "Your best friend moved away and you miss them very much." Try to think of situations that kids can relate to and that might cause them to feel upset or disappointed.

2. **Introduce the Activity:** Explain to the kids that they will be acting out different scenarios and practicing using their distress tolerance skills. Remind them that it's okay to feel upset sometimes, but the goal is to learn how to manage those feelings in a healthy way.

3. **Role-Play:** Have each child pick a scenario card. Give them a few minutes to think about how they would react in that situation and what distress tolerance skills they could use. They can choose to use distraction, self-soothing, or any other distress tolerance technique they've learned.

4. **Act It Out:** One by one, have each child act out their scenario and show how they would use distress tolerance skills to handle the situation. Encourage them to be as creative as they like. Other kids can take on supporting roles if needed.

5. **Discuss:** After each role-play, discuss as a group. What did the child do well? What other strategies could they have used? How did it feel to use distress tolerance skills?

6. **Reflection:** At the end of the activity, have each child share something they learned about distress tolerance. What will they do differently next time they face a tough situation? How can they use what they've learned in their daily lives?

Remember, the goal of this activity is not to avoid or suppress negative emotions, but to handle them in a more effective way. Praise kids for their efforts and for trying out new strategies, and remind them that it's okay to ask for help when they're upset. It's all part of learning and growing!

Exercise: Distress Tolerance Scenario Worksheet

Objective: This worksheet is designed to reinforce the concept of distress tolerance and help kids apply these skills in various situations.

Materials Needed: Printed worksheets, pens or pencils.

The worksheet could be structured as follows:

Distress Tolerance Scenario Worksheet

Name: _____ **Date:** _____

Instructions: Read each scenario below. Then, write down what you could do to practice distress tolerance in that situation. Remember, you can use strategies like distraction, self-soothing, and asking for help. There are no wrong answers – just try your best!

1. **Scenario:** You worked really hard on a project for school, but you didn't get the grade you were hoping for.

   - **What I Could Do:**

2. **Scenario:** Your best friend is moving to another city, and you're going to miss them a lot.

   - **What I Could Do:**

3. **Scenario:** You were supposed to have a fun day at the park, but it started raining and you had to stay inside.

   - **What I Could Do:**

4. **Scenario:** Your little brother broke your favorite toy.

- **What I Could Do:**

---

5. **Scenario:** You tried out for the soccer team but didn't make it.

- **What I Could Do:**

Remember, practicing distress tolerance is like exercising a muscle – the more you do it, the stronger you get! Keep practicing, and you'll become a real-life superhero in handling tough situations!

This worksheet offers a valuable opportunity for kids to reflect on their own reactions and think of ways they can apply distress tolerance skills. It also provides a chance for adults to understand the child's thought process and offer guidance where needed.

Skills for Distress Tolerance

Imagine you're playing a really difficult level on your favorite video game. You've been trying to beat it for ages, but you just can't seem to win. You start to feel really frustrated and upset. What do you do? Do you throw your game controller? Do you give up and stop playing forever? Or do you find a way to calm down and keep trying?

This is where Distress Tolerance skills can help. They're like special tools that help you handle tough situations without losing your cool. Let's think about what these tools might look like:

1. Self-Soothing: Imagine if you had a magic blanket that could make you feel better whenever you're upset. Self-soothing is like that magic blanket. It's all about doing things that make you feel calm and safe. This could be listening to your favorite music, cuddling with a soft toy, or smelling a scent you love, like fresh cookies or flowers.

2. Distraction: Sometimes, the best way to handle a tough situation is to take your mind off it for a while. That's what distraction is all about. You could draw a picture, read a funny comic, or play with your pet. After a while, you might find that you feel better and can think more clearly about the problem.

3. Improving the Moment: This tool is about finding a way to make the present moment a little bit better. Maybe you can't change the hard thing that's happening, but you can change how you feel about it. You could imagine a peaceful place, tell yourself encouraging words, or do something kind that helps someone else.

4. Radical Acceptance: This one might sound a bit weird at first. Radical acceptance is about saying to yourself, "Yes, this is happening, and I can't change it." Sometimes, we spend so much energy fighting against things we can't change that it only makes us more upset. With radical acceptance, we learn to let go and save our energy for things we can change.

Remember, it's okay to feel upset or frustrated. Everyone does sometimes! But with these Distress Tolerance skills, you can help yourself feel better and get through tough times. Just like that difficult video game level, with practice and patience, you can get better at using these skills and overcoming challenges. And who knows? Maybe the game level that seemed so hard before will be a piece of cake next time!

Activity: Create a Personal Soothe Box

Objective: To help kids learn about self-soothing and create a personalized tool they can use when they're feeling upset or distressed.

Materials:

- A box (it can be a shoe box, a gift box, or any other box you like)

- Art supplies for decorating the box (like paint, stickers, glitter, etc.)

- Items to put in the box that can help soothe. These will be different for everyone but can include things like:

    - A soft toy or blanket

    - A picture of a happy memory or loved ones

    - A favorite book or comic

    - A notebook and colorful pens for writing or drawing

    - A music playlist or a favorite song

    - Some nice smelling lotion or a scented candle

    - A stress ball or squishy toy

Instructions:

1. **Decorate Your Box:** Make your Soothe Box special! Use paint, stickers, glitter, or anything else you like to decorate the outside of your box. You can write your name on it, draw pictures, or anything else that makes you happy.

2. **Choose Your Soothing Items:** Think about the things that make you feel calm and happy when you're upset. Is there a song that always makes you smile? A picture that reminds you of a fun day? A blanket that feels super soft? Choose a few of these things to put in your box.

3. **Fill Your Box:** Put your soothing items inside the box. You might want to arrange them in a special way, or just put them in however you like. It's your box, so you get to decide!

4. **Use Your Box:** Next time you're feeling upset, open your Soothe Box and use the items inside to help you feel better. Remember, it's okay to feel upset sometimes, and it's great to take care of yourself when you do.

Discussion: After the activity, discuss how it felt to create and use the Soothe Box. What items did you choose, and why? How did using the Soothe Box help you when you were upset?

Remember, everyone's Soothe Box will be different because everyone is unique. That's what makes each Soothe Box special. It's a box full of all the things that help YOU feel better, and that's pretty cool!

Exercise: Practice Using Distress Tolerance Skills

Objective: The goal of this exercise is to help kids understand and practice using Distress Tolerance skills in different situations.

Materials:

- Scenario cards: These are index cards with different scenarios written on them that might cause distress. Make sure the scenarios are age-appropriate and relevant to the child's experiences. Examples might include: "You got a lower grade than you expected on a test," "Your best friend moved away," "You had a fight with your sibling," etc.

- A worksheet with a list of Distress Tolerance skills from the chapter (Self-Soothing, Distraction, Improving the Moment, Radical Acceptance) and space to write down how they might use each skill in the scenario.

Instructions:

1. **Choose a Scenario Card:** Pick one of the scenario cards. Read it and imagine that this situation is happening to you. How would you feel?

2. **Identify Distress Tolerance Skills:** Look at your worksheet. Which of the Distress Tolerance skills do you think you could use in this situation? You might be able to use more than one!

3. **Practice Using the Skills:** Write down how you could use each Distress Tolerance skill you chose in the scenario. For example, if your scenario is "You got a lower grade than you expected on a test," you might write:

   - Self-Soothing: "I could listen to my favorite music to help calm down."

   - Distraction: "I could read my favorite book to take my mind off the grade for a while."

- Improving the Moment: "I could remind myself that one grade doesn't define me and that I can learn from this and improve."

- Radical Acceptance: "I could accept that I got a lower grade than I wanted and understand that it's okay to be upset about it."

4. **Reflect:** After you've written down your answers, think about how using these skills might change how you feel in the scenario. Do you think it would help you handle the situation better?

Discussion: After completing the exercise, discuss how it felt to think about using Distress Tolerance skills in different scenarios. Which skills do you think would be most helpful to you in real life? Remember, it's okay to prefer some skills over others. The important thing is finding what works best for you!

CHAPTER 5: EMOTIONAL REGULATION

Understanding Emotional Regulation

Hello, friends! You know how some days you feel as happy as a dolphin diving through sparkling waves, and other times you might feel as grumpy as a bear who missed breakfast? Those feelings that bubble up inside of us? Those are called emotions. All of us have them, and they're a completely normal part of being human.

Now, imagine if we could be the captains of our emotional ship. Steering our feelings so that we don't get tossed around when the emotional sea gets a little stormy. Well, guess what? We can! And this superpower is called 'Emotional Regulation.'

Emotional Regulation sounds like a big, fancy term, but it's just a way of talking about how we manage our feelings. Just like how we might clean up our room when it gets messy, emotional regulation means tidying up our feelings when they feel a little topsy-turvy.

It's about noticing how you're feeling and then deciding what to do with that feeling. For example, if you're feeling as angry as a hornet's nest, emotional regulation might help you take a few deep breaths or count to ten, instead of stomping your feet or shouting. Or if you're feeling super excited, like a puppy with a new toy, emotional regulation might remind you to not disturb others who are busy or resting.

Sometimes, our feelings can be a bit like weather. You know how some days are sunny and calm, but other days can be stormy and wild? Emotional regulation is like having an umbrella for when it's raining, a hat for when it's sunny, and a cozy jacket for when it's chilly. It doesn't stop the weather from happening, but it helps us deal with whatever the day brings!

Just remember, it's perfectly okay to have strong feelings. In fact, it's normal! But emotional regulation is there to help us handle them in the best way possible. It's like having a toolkit for your feelings, filled with tools like deep breathing, counting to ten, talking to a friend, or hugging a teddy bear. All these tools can help us feel a bit more balanced.

So, the next time you feel a big, powerful emotion coming on, remember your superpower: Emotional Regulation. Take a deep breath, reach for your toolkit, and remember - you're the captain of your emotional ship!

This explanation aims to describe Emotional Regulation in a fun, relatable, and straightforward manner. It uses metaphors and examples that children can easily understand, and it emphasizes the positive and empowering aspects of Emotional Regulation.

Activity: Emotion Thermometer Craft

Emotion Thermometer Craft Activity

Materials:

1. A long piece of construction paper (preferably red)
2. A piece of white cardstock or heavy paper
3. Markers or colored pencils
4. Glue or tape
5. Scissors
6. A ruler
7. Stickers or pictures (optional)

Instructions:

1. **Prepare your materials:** Gather all your materials together in your workspace. Make sure you have everything you need before you start.

2. **Make the thermometer:** Take the long piece of red construction paper and cut it into a long, thin strip, about an inch wide and the length of the paper.

3. **Create the scale:** Draw a line down the middle of the white cardstock paper. Use the ruler to mark off even spaces along the line. These will represent different levels of emotions.

4. **Label the emotions:** At the bottom of the line, write "Calm" or "Relaxed." This represents when we are feeling at ease. As you move up the line, label the spaces with other emotions like "Happy," "Excited," "Annoyed," "Angry," all the way up to "Furious" at the top. You can choose any emotions that make sense to you - there's no right or wrong!

5. **Add the thermometer:** Now, stick the red strip of construction paper on the line you drew. This is your "emotion level" that can move up and down.

6. **Decorate your thermometer:** Use your markers, colored pencils, and stickers to decorate your emotion thermometer. You could draw faces

showing each emotion next to the labels, or color in each section a different color.

7. **Practice using your thermometer:** Think about different scenarios and decide where your feelings would land on your emotion thermometer. For example, if your brother took your toy without asking, where would your emotion level rise to? What about if you're playing your favorite game?

Remember, everyone's emotion thermometer will look different because we all experience emotions in our own way. It's okay if your thermometer doesn't look exactly like your friend's. The important thing is that it helps you understand your feelings better!

Through this activity, kids will be able to visually represent their feelings and understand that emotions can vary in intensity. This is a crucial aspect of emotional regulation.

Exercise: Emotional Regulation Practice Worksheet

The worksheet could be divided into several sections, each representing a different scenario that might trigger strong emotions. For each scenario, there would be a series of questions or activities to help the child practice emotional regulation.

Section 1: Scenario

The first part of each section would present a scenario that could trigger an emotional response. For example:

- "Imagine you're playing a game, and someone else wins. How do you feel?"

Section 2: Identifying Emotions

The next part would ask the child to identify their emotions in that scenario. They could choose from a list of emotions or write their own. For example:

- "Circle the emotions you might feel: Happy, Sad, Angry, Excited, Frustrated, Jealous, Other: ____"

Section 3: Rating Emotions

The third part would ask the child to rate the intensity of their emotions on a scale from 1 to 10 (with 1 being very mild and 10 being very intense). They could use their Emotion Thermometer from the previous activity to help them with this.

- "Using your Emotion Thermometer, rate how strongly you feel the emotion: ____"

Section 4: Choosing a Regulation Strategy

The fourth part would present a list of emotional regulation strategies, and the child would choose which one(s) they could use in the given scenario. For example:

- "Which emotional regulation strategies could you use? Circle all that apply: Take deep breaths, Count to ten, Talk to a friend, Take a break, Other: ____"

Section 5: Reflecting on the Outcome

The final part would ask the child to reflect on the potential outcome of using the chosen emotional regulation strategies. For example:

- "How might you feel after using these strategies? _____"

This worksheet would provide kids with a practical tool to practice emotional regulation in various scenarios. By thinking through these situations in advance, they will be better prepared to handle their emotions when they face similar situations in real life

Techniques for Emotional Regulation

Have you ever felt like your emotions are so big and powerful, like a giant wave in the ocean? Sometimes, it might seem like they're in control, not you. But guess what? You're the boss of your feelings, not the other way around! This is where "emotional regulation" comes in.

Emotional regulation is like being the captain of your very own emotion-ship. Imagine that your feelings are the sea. Sometimes the sea is calm and peaceful, other times it's stormy and rough. As the captain, you can't control the sea, but you can learn to steer your ship in any weather. That's exactly what emotional regulation helps you do!

Now, let's learn about some cool techniques to help you navigate through your ocean of feelings.

1. **Deep Breathing:** Remember when you blow bubbles with your bubble wand? Deep breathing is just like that. When your emotions feel too big, take a deep breath in, hold it for a moment, and then let it out slowly, like you're blowing a giant bubble. This helps calm your body and mind, just like the ocean after a storm.

2. **Mindful Moments:** Imagine you're a detective and your job is to notice everything around you. What do you see? What do you hear? What do you smell? Paying attention to what's happening right now can help take your mind off overwhelming feelings and bring you back to the present moment.

3. **Emotion Detective:** Sometimes, feelings can be confusing. They can be like a tangled ball of yarn. Being an emotion detective means you try to figure out what you're feeling and why. Maybe you're not angry at your little sister; you're just tired after a long day. Figuring out your real feelings can help you understand them better.

4. **Positive Self-Talk:** Remember, you're the captain of your emotion-ship, and captains are brave and kind. So, speak to yourself like a captain would. If

you're feeling scared, tell yourself, "It's okay to be scared, but I'm brave too." Or if you're sad, remind yourself, "It's okay to feel sad, I know it won't last forever." This is called positive self-talk, and it can help you feel better when you're going through tough times.

5. **Expressing Your Feelings:** Sometimes, the best way to deal with big feelings is to let them out. You can talk to someone you trust about how you feel, write about it in a diary, or express it through a drawing or a dance. When you share your feelings, they often start to feel a bit smaller and more manageable.

6. **The Pause Button:** When your feelings are very strong, imagine you have a pause button like on a video game. Hit that button, take a break, and give yourself some time to think before you react. This can prevent your big feelings from taking control of your actions.

Remember, it's okay to have big feelings, and it's okay if you don't get it right all the time. You're learning, and that's what matters most. You're a great emotion-ship captain in the making!

Activity: Create an Emotion Regulation Plan

Objective: To help kids understand their emotions better and come up with strategies to manage them.

Materials needed:

- A sheet of paper

- Colored pencils, markers, or crayons

- Stickers or any other art supplies (optional)

Steps:

1. **Identify Your Feelings**: Draw a big circle in the center of your paper and divide it into slices like a pizza or a pie. Each slice represents a different emotion. Color each slice with a different color and label it with an emotion you often feel. These could include feelings like happiness, sadness, anger, fear, excitement, etc.

2. **When Do You Feel This Way?**: Under each emotion, write down times when you usually feel that way. Maybe you feel happy when you're playing with your friends, or you feel angry when you have to do chores you don't like.

3. **How Does Your Body React?**: Next to each emotion, draw a small stick figure. Around this figure, write or draw how your body reacts when you feel this emotion. For instance, when you're scared, your heart might beat faster, or when you're angry, you might clench your fists.

4. **Your Personal Coping Strategies**: Now, for each emotion, think about what helps you feel better when you're experiencing it. Draw a line from each emotion to the edge of your paper and create a box there. In each box, write or draw the coping strategies that work for you. Maybe when you're sad, hugging your teddy bear helps. Or when you're angry, counting to ten slowly helps you calm down.

5. **Ask for Help**: At the bottom of your paper, draw a big heart. Inside it, write down the names of people you can talk to when your feelings feel too big to handle alone. This could include parents, siblings, teachers, or friends. Remember, it's okay to ask for help!

At the end of this activity, you'll have your own Emotion Regulation Plan, which is like a map guiding you through your emotions. Whenever you're feeling a certain way, you can refer to your plan to help you understand and manage your feelings better. It's okay if some strategies don't always work. The important thing is to keep trying and exploring what works best for you. After all, you're the captain of your emotion-ship!

Exercise: Emotion Regulation Skills Practice

Objective: To provide kids with the opportunity to apply their emotion regulation skills in different scenarios.

Materials needed:

- A piece of paper

- A pencil or pen

Instructions:

1. **Create Scenarios**: Write down 5-7 different scenarios that can trigger strong emotions. For instance, "Your best friend didn't invite you to their birthday party", or "You scored the winning goal in a soccer match".

2. **Identify Emotions**: For each scenario, identify the emotion that you would feel. Would you feel angry, sad, surprised, happy, or something else?

3. **Body Reactions**: Think about how your body would react in each scenario. Would your heart beat faster? Would your palms get sweaty? Write it down.

4. **Use Your Emotion Regulation Plan**: Now, refer to your Emotion Regulation Plan from the previous activity. Choose a coping strategy from your plan that you think would be helpful in each scenario. It's okay if you want to come up with a new coping strategy that's not in your plan.

5. **Reflect**: After going through all the scenarios, think about how you felt during this exercise. Was it easy or hard to choose a coping strategy for each scenario? Were there any scenarios that felt particularly difficult?

Note: This is a practice exercise, so it's okay if you don't have all the answers. The important thing is to keep practicing your emotion regulation skills. Remember, you're learning to be the captain of your emotion-ship, and every captain needs practice!

The purpose of this exercise is to help children understand how different situations can trigger different emotions, and how they can use their emotional regulation skills to manage their reactions to these situations.

CHAPTER 6: INTERPERSONAL EFFECTIVENESS

Understanding Interpersonal Effectiveness

Today, we're going to talk about something really important. It's called Interpersonal Effectiveness. Big words, right? But don't worry, it's not as complicated as it sounds.

So, what does 'Interpersonal Effectiveness' mean? Well, 'interpersonal' means between people, and 'effectiveness' means doing something well. So, Interpersonal Effectiveness is all about how well we interact or communicate with others, including our friends, family, and teachers.

Imagine you're playing a game with your friends, and you all have different ideas about the rules. Or think about a time when you really wanted a pet, but your parents weren't sure. How did you handle these situations? Did you yell or pout? Did you listen and talk calmly? Or maybe you didn't know what to do at all.

Interpersonal Effectiveness is like a tool kit that helps you handle these situations better. It's about learning to express your thoughts, needs, and feelings in a way that's respectful to others and to yourself. It's also about listening to others and understanding their point of view.

But why is this important? Well, using Interpersonal Effectiveness skills can help us have healthier relationships. It can also help us feel more understood, less frustrated, and happier overall. Plus, it's a great way to solve problems and disagreements without hurting anyone's feelings.

Here are some key parts of Interpersonal Effectiveness:

1. **Understanding your needs and feelings**: Before you can express your feelings to others, you need to understand them yourself. It's like trying to explain a movie to a friend when you haven't watched it yet.

2. **Expressing yourself clearly**: Once you understand your feelings, you need to share them. And not just by talking louder! It's about choosing the right words and tone of voice.

3. **Listening to others**: Interpersonal Effectiveness is a two-way street. It's not just about talking, but also about listening to what others have to say.

4. **Problem-solving**: Sometimes, people have different wants or opinions, and that's okay. The key is to find a solution that works for everyone. It's like putting together a puzzle where everyone's pieces fit.

Remember, everyone makes mistakes and that's okay. It's all part of learning. The important thing is to keep trying and to use these skills a little bit more each day. Pretty soon, you'll be a master at Interpersonal Effectiveness, and you'll notice how much easier and happier your interactions with others can be.

So, are you ready to start practicing your super communication skills? We believe in you!

Activity: Interpersonal Effectiveness Skits

Objective: To understand and practice Interpersonal Effectiveness through role-play.

Materials Needed:

- Small pieces of paper or index cards

- Pens or pencils

- A box or hat to draw from

Steps:

1. **Setting Up**: Write down different scenarios on pieces of paper. These scenarios should involve two or more people and a situation where interpersonal skills are needed. For example:

   - "You want to borrow a book from your friend, but they're not finished reading it yet."

   - "Your sibling took your toy without asking."

   - "Your friend wants to play a game you don't like."

   - "Your parent asks you to do your homework, but you want to watch TV."

2. **Choosing Roles**: Divide the kids into pairs or small groups. Let each group pick a scenario from the box or hat. Once they have their scenario, have them decide who will play which role.

3. **Planning the Skit**: Give each group some time to plan out their skit. They should think about how they can use interpersonal effectiveness skills in their scenario. Encourage them to think about understanding feelings, expressing themselves clearly, listening, and problem-solving.

4. **Performing the Skit**: Once they've planned their skits, it's showtime! Let each group perform their skit for everyone else. Make sure everyone gets a chance to act.

5. **Discussing the Skit**: After each skit, have a group discussion. Ask questions like:

- "What did you notice about how the characters communicated?"
- "What interpersonal effectiveness skills did they use?"
- "What could they have done differently?"
- "How did the situation get resolved?"

6. **Reflection**: Finally, have each kid share one thing they learned from this activity that they can use in their own lives.

By acting out these skits and discussing them, kids can learn about and practice Interpersonal Effectiveness in a fun and engaging way. It also helps them see how these skills can be used in real-life situations.

Exercise: Interpersonal Effectiveness Reflection

Objective: To reflect on the use of Interpersonal Effectiveness skills in real-life situations and to promote self-awareness.

Materials Needed:

- A copy of the "Interpersonal Effectiveness Reflection Worksheet" for each child

- Pens or pencils

Interpersonal Effectiveness Reflection Worksheet:

1. **Think about a time when you interacted with someone else** (like a friend, sibling, or parent). Write down what happened:

2. **Did you express your thoughts and feelings clearly?** If yes, how did you do it? If not, how could you do it better?

3. **Did you listen to the other person's thoughts and feelings?** If yes, how did you show that you were listening? If not, what could you do differently next time?

4. **Did you try to understand the other person's point of view?** If yes, how did it help the situation? If not, why do you think it's important to do so?

5. **How did you try to solve the problem or disagreement (if there was one)?** Do you think it was effective? Why or why not?

6. **What is one thing you learned from this situation about Interpersonal Effectiveness?** How can you use this lesson in the future?

Steps:

1. **Hand Out the Worksheet**: Give each kid a copy of the "Interpersonal Effectiveness Reflection Worksheet" and a pen or pencil.

2. **Complete the Worksheet**: Give the kids some time to fill out their worksheets. Encourage them to think carefully about their responses and to be honest with themselves.

3. **Group Discussion (Optional)**: If appropriate and the kids are comfortable with it, you can have a group discussion where they share their answers. Make sure to foster a supportive and non-judgmental environment.

This reflection exercise can provide valuable insights for the kids about their own Interpersonal Effectiveness skills, their strengths, areas for improvement, and how they can apply these skills in future interactions.

Skills for Interpersonal Effectiveness

Today we're going to learn about something really cool - Skills for Interpersonal Effectiveness. That's a big phrase, isn't it? But don't worry, we're going to break it down and make it as easy as pie!

So, what does "interpersonal effectiveness" mean? Let's take it word by word. "Inter" means between, and "personal" means people - so "interpersonal" is all about what happens between people. And "effectiveness" means being really good at doing something.

Put them together and you get "interpersonal effectiveness" - being really good at dealing with people. It's about having great friendships, getting along well with your family, and even dealing with people who aren't so friendly to you.

Now, how do we get good at this? Here are a few skills that can help.

1. Understand and Respect Others: This means trying to see things from the other person's point of view and respecting their feelings, even if you don't agree with them. Remember, it's like wearing their shoes for a bit to see how it feels.

2. Express Your Feelings Clearly: It's important to tell people how you feel, but in a kind way. If your friend took your toy without asking, you might say, "I felt upset when you took my toy without asking. Can you please ask next time?"

3. Listen Carefully: When someone is talking to you, show them you're interested. Look at them, nod your head, and respond to what they're saying. It shows you respect them and their feelings.

4. Say No When Needed: Sometimes, we need to say "no" to protect ourselves or our time. And that's okay! Remember, you have the right to your own time and space.

5. Cooperate and Compromise: Life isn't always about winning. Sometimes, we need to work together with others and find a middle ground. If you and your friend want to play different games, maybe you can play both, one after the other!

These skills might seem tough at first, but remember, even the biggest, toughest tasks get easier with practice. And the great thing about these skills? You can practice them anywhere - at school, at home, at the park, anywhere you interact with people!

Remember, nobody's perfect, and everyone is learning. If you don't get it right the first time, that's okay! The most important thing is to keep trying and keep learning. So go on, get out there, and be the superstar you're meant to be!

Activity: Friendship Building Activities

Activity 1: "Two Truths and a Lie" Ice Breaker

Objective: Improve communication and learn more about each other.

Instructions:

1. Each child should think of two true facts about themselves and one false one.

2. Everyone takes turns sharing their three "facts". The rest of the group tries to guess which one is the lie.

Activity 2: Team Puzzle Challenge

Objective: Promote cooperation and teamwork.

Instructions:

1. Divide the kids into small groups.

2. Give each group a puzzle to solve.

3. The goal is not just to finish the puzzle, but to make sure every team member contributes to the solution. They can take turns adding pieces, or work together to find the next piece.

Activity 3: Compliment Circles

Objective: Enhance appreciation and positivity in relationships.

Instructions:

1. Have the kids sit in a circle.

2. One child starts by giving a compliment to the person on their right. It could be about their appearance, something they're good at, or a nice thing they did.

3. The complimented child then compliments the next person, and so on, until everyone has received and given a compliment.

Activity 4: Friendship Bracelet Making

Objective: Encourage creativity and sharing while building a sense of belonging.

Instructions:

1. Provide a variety of beads, strings, and other materials.

2. Each child makes two bracelets - one to keep and one to give to a friend.

3. After making the bracelets, each child shares why they chose the design or colors for their friend's bracelet.

Activity 5: Role-Play Scenarios

Objective: Practice conflict resolution and effective communication.

Instructions:

1. Create various scenarios where friends might have disagreements or misunderstandings (e.g., wanting to play different games, having a misunderstanding, etc.)

2. Have pairs of kids role-play these scenarios and practice using their interpersonal effectiveness skills to resolve the conflicts.

Remember, the goal of these activities is not just to have fun, but also to practice and improve interpersonal effectiveness skills. So make sure to discuss and reflect on each activity afterwards, talking about what went well and what can be improved for next time.

Exercise: Interpersonal Skills Practice

Exercise 1: Feelings Charades

Objective: Improve empathy and understanding of emotions.

Instructions:

1. Write different emotions on pieces of paper and put them in a bowl.

2. Have kids take turns picking a paper and acting out the emotion without using words.

3. The rest of the group guesses the emotion.

Exercise 2: Active Listening Checklist

Objective: Enhance listening skills.

Instructions:

1. Make a checklist of active listening behaviors, such as: making eye contact, nodding in agreement, asking relevant questions, and summarizing what the other person said.

2. Have kids pair up and take turns talking about a topic of their choice. The listener uses the checklist to practice active listening.

3. After both kids have had a chance to speak and listen, they can discuss how it felt to be listened to attentively.

Exercise 3: Assertive Communication Practice

Objective: Practice expressing feelings and wants respectfully.

Instructions:

1. Prepare some scenarios where the child needs to express a feeling or request. For example, "Your friend borrowed your favorite book and hasn't returned it."

2. Ask the child to use "I" statements to express their feelings or wants. For example, "I feel upset because I haven't gotten my book back. Can you please return it tomorrow?"

Exercise 4: Problem-Solving Scenarios

Objective: Enhance problem-solving and decision-making skills.

Instructions:

1. Write different scenarios involving interpersonal conflicts on pieces of paper and put them in a bowl.

2. Have kids draw a scenario and brainstorm possible solutions. Encourage them to think about the consequences of each solution.

3. After they choose a solution, discuss why they chose it and how they think it would work.

Exercise 5: Reflective Journaling

Objective: Foster self-awareness and understanding of interpersonal interactions.

Instructions:

1. At the end of each day, have the kids write in a journal about their interpersonal interactions. They can write about what went well, what they struggled with, and what they learned.

2. Encourage them to also write about how they can apply what they've learned in future interactions.

These exercises can be adjusted according to the kids' ages and developmental levels. The important thing is to ensure that they understand the concepts and are able to apply the skills in their everyday lives.

CHAPTER 7: BALANCING ACCEPTANCE AND CHANGE

Understanding Acceptance and Change

Have you ever tried to hold a squiggly worm in your hand? Or keep a lively puppy still? It's not easy, right? Some things just don't stay still, no matter how hard you try. And that's a little bit like life. Life is always changing, moving, and growing, just like that worm or that puppy. And just like you!

In life, there are things we can control, like choosing our clothes, brushing our teeth, or picking a book to read. And then there are things we can't control, like the weather, getting a cold, or how other people behave. Trying to control things that we can't change can make us feel frustrated and unhappy. This is where "acceptance" comes in.

Acceptance is like saying, "Okay, this is how things are right now, and that's okay." It's not about giving up or saying that everything is perfect. It's about understanding that some things are the way they are, and that's okay.

Imagine it's a rainy day and you wanted to go play outside. You can't change the weather, can you? But you can accept it. You might say, "Okay, it's raining. I can't go outside to play, but I can find something fun to do inside instead." That's acceptance!

Now, what about change? Change is a part of life, too. You change as you grow older. The seasons change. Even your feelings change. And change can be good! It's because of change that you learn new things, make new friends, and have new experiences.

But change can also be tough sometimes. Like when you have to move to a new school or when you're learning a new skill. Change can feel scary or uncomfortable. But remember, it's okay to feel this way. Everyone does when faced with change.

To make change easier, it's important to remember that it's okay to go slow, ask for help, and take care of yourself. It's like learning to ride a bike. At first, it might feel scary and you might fall. But with practice, patience, and maybe some help, you'll eventually learn to ride.

So, acceptance and change are two big parts of life. Acceptance is about understanding what we can't change, and being okay with it. And change, even though it can be tough sometimes, helps us grow and learn new things.

Activity: Balancing Act Game

Materials Needed:

- A flat board (like a piece of cardboard or a book)

- Small objects of various weights and sizes (like blocks, marbles, or stuffed toys)

- A round object (like a ball or a rolled-up sock) to act as the fulcrum (the balancing point)

Instructions:

1. Set up your balancing board by placing the round object under the middle of the board. Now, you've got your own seesaw!

2. Gather all the small objects and divide them into two groups: one group to represent things we can change (like our actions or our attitudes), and the other to represent things we can't change (like the weather or other people's feelings).

3. Now, take turns placing objects from each group on either side of the balancing board. Try to keep the board balanced. Remember, this represents how we need to balance acceptance (of things we can't change) and change (of things we can control) in our lives.

4. If the board tips too much to one side, discuss what could be done to bring it back into balance. Do we need to accept something we can't change? Or is there something we can change to make things better?

5. Keep playing until all the objects have been placed on the board. Did you manage to keep it balanced? If not, that's okay! In life, it's normal for things to get out of balance sometimes. The important thing is that we keep trying and learning.

Discussion:

After the game, have a chat about what you learned. Discuss how sometimes we try to control things that are out of our control, and how this can lead to frustration. Talk about how accepting what we can't change, and focusing on what we can change, can help us feel more balanced and less stressed.

This "Balancing Act Game" is a fun and interactive way to help kids understand the concepts of acceptance and change. It's a hands-on way to show how trying to control things outside our control can throw us off balance, and how acceptance can help restore that balance. It also emphasizes that it's okay if things aren't perfectly balanced all the time, as long as we keep learning and trying.

Exercise: Acceptance and Change Scenario Worksheet

This exercise consists of various scenarios. For each scenario, identify what parts can be accepted (things that can't be changed) and what parts can be changed (things that you can control).

1. **Scenario: It's raining and you planned to have a picnic outside.**

   - Acceptance:

   - Change:

2. **Scenario: You are moving to a new school and feeling nervous.**

   - Acceptance:

   - Change:

3. **Scenario: You didn't do well on a math test.**

   - Acceptance:

   - Change:

4. **Scenario: Your best friend is moving away.**

   - Acceptance:

   - Change:

5. **Scenario: You're feeling bored at home during the summer holidays.**

   - Acceptance:

   - Change:

Hint: Remember, the things we can accept are usually outside of our control (like the weather, other people's actions, etc.). The things we can change are usually within our control (like our actions, our attitudes, etc.).

After you've filled out the worksheet, discuss your answers with a parent, teacher, or friend. This can help you understand better how to apply acceptance and change in different situations.

This exercise will help children think through various scenarios and identify what aspects they can and cannot change, promoting a better understanding of the concepts of acceptance and change.

Practicing Acceptance and Change

"Have you ever tried to hold a beach ball under water at the pool? It's tough, isn't it? The ball keeps popping back up no matter how hard you try to keep it down. In a way, our feelings can be like that beach ball. When we try to push them away or ignore them, they keep popping back up. This is where acceptance comes in. Acceptance is like letting the beach ball float on the water. It doesn't mean you like the ball or want it there; it just means you're letting it be there without trying to push it away.

Imagine you're feeling really upset because your best friend moved away. Trying to pretend you're not sad wouldn't help much, would it? But what if you could say to yourself, "I'm really sad, and that's okay. It's normal to feel this way when a friend moves away." That's acceptance!

Now, let's talk about change. Change is when something becomes different. Change can be exciting, like when you lose a tooth and know the tooth fairy is coming! But change can also be hard, like when you have to move to a new school. Change can feel scary because we don't know what's going to happen next.

But remember, change also means that things won't stay the same forever. That sad feeling you have because your friend moved away? It won't last forever. Over time, it will change. You'll start to feel a little less sad. You might make a new friend. Or maybe you'll get to visit your old friend.

Practicing acceptance and change is like being a brave explorer on an adventure. You might not know what's coming next, but you're ready to face it. Acceptance is like your shield, helping you to handle tough feelings. Change is like your magic map, reminding you that things won't always stay the same.

And remember, it's okay to ask for help. Just like an explorer might need help reading their map or carrying their shield, it's okay to ask for help when you're dealing with tough feelings or big changes. Talking to a grown-up you trust, like a parent or teacher, can be a great way to practice acceptance and change.

So, the next time you're feeling a strong emotion or facing a big change, remember your shield of acceptance and your map of change. Know that it's okay to feel what you're feeling and that those feelings will change over time. And don't forget, every brave explorer needs a team, so don't be afraid to ask for help when you need it."

Activity: Acceptance and Change Art Project

Materials:

1. Art paper or canvas

2. Paints and brushes (or any other art supplies like colored pencils, crayons, or markers)

3. Glue

4. Old magazines, newspapers, or printed images (optional)

5. Scissors

Instructions:

Part 1 - Acceptance

1. Think about a feeling or situation that you're finding hard to accept. It could be a feeling like sadness or anger, or a situation like moving to a new school or a friend moving away.

2. Using your art supplies, draw or paint a picture of this feeling or situation on one side of your paper or canvas. You could use colors, shapes, or even make a collage with cut-out pictures from your magazines or newspapers to represent your feeling or situation.

3. As you create your artwork, remember that it's okay to feel these feelings or have these experiences. This is your acceptance art!

Part 2 - Change

4. Now, think about how this feeling or situation might change over time. Maybe you will start to feel happier or calmer. Maybe your new school will start to feel more like home. Or maybe you'll make a new friend.

5. On the other side of your paper or canvas, create an art piece that represents this change. Again, you can use colors, shapes, or a collage to show how things might change.

6. As you're working on your art, remind yourself that things don't stay the same forever and that change is a part of life. This is your change art!

Part 3 - Reflection

7. When you're done, take a look at both sides of your art project. One side shows acceptance and the other side shows change.

8. Talk about your art project with a grown-up you trust. You can tell them about what your art represents and how it helped you understand acceptance and change better.

Exercise: Personal Acceptance and Change Journaling

Materials:

1. A journal or notebook

2. A pen or pencil

Instructions:

Part 1 - Acceptance

1. Think about a situation or feeling that you're finding hard to accept. It could be a change in your life, a problem you're facing, or a strong emotion you're experiencing.

2. Write about this situation or feeling in your journal. Try to describe it as honestly and completely as you can.

3. Now, write a letter to yourself about this situation or feeling. In this letter, remind yourself that it's okay to feel this way or to be in this situation. This is your way of practicing acceptance.

Part 2 - Change

4. Next, think about how this situation or feeling might change over time. How do you hope it will change? What could be different in the future?

5. Write about these changes in your journal. Imagine you're writing a story about your future, where these changes have happened.

6. As you're writing, remind yourself that things can and will change. This is your way of recognizing and embracing change.

Part 3 - Reflection

7. Finally, take some time to reflect on what you've written. How does it feel to practice acceptance? How does it feel to think about change?

8. You can write about your reflections in your journal. You can also choose to share your thoughts with a trusted adult, if you're comfortable doing so.

This exercise allows kids to engage with their feelings and thoughts on a deeper level, and it provides a safe space to express themselves. Remember, there's no right or wrong answers here. It's all about exploring your own feelings and experiences with acceptance and change.

CHAPTER 8: SELF-CARE AND DBT

The Importance of Self-Care

Imagine your body is like a shiny, new car. What happens if you don't take good care of it? If you never wash it, never check the oil, or never fill it up with gas? Well, over time, that shiny new car won't look so shiny anymore. It might even stop running altogether!

Our bodies are a lot like cars. They need proper care to keep running smoothly. This is where self-care comes into play. It's just like taking care of a car, but instead, it's taking care of our own bodies and minds!

Self-care is doing things that make you feel good and keep you healthy. It's not just about brushing your teeth or combing your hair, even though those things are important. Self-care also includes doing activities that help us relax, make us happy, and keep our minds sharp.

When we take care of ourselves, we feel better. We can concentrate better in school, we're nicer to our friends and family, and we can handle tough situations more easily. Plus, doing self-care activities can be a lot of fun!

Think about the things that make you feel good. Maybe it's reading a book, playing a game, drawing a picture, or spending time with your pet. These are all examples of self-care because they help you relax and feel happy.

But self-care also includes things that might not always be fun but are still very important, like eating healthy food, getting plenty of sleep, and exercising regularly. It's kind of like when you have to put gas in the car. It might not be the most fun thing to do, but if you don't do it, the car won't go anywhere!

Remember, everyone's self-care routine is different. Your best friend might love to go for a run to feel good, but maybe you prefer to read a book instead. That's okay! The most important thing is that you're doing what makes you feel happy and healthy.

So, why is self-care so important? Well, just like that shiny new car, we want our bodies and minds to keep running smoothly for a long time. Taking care of ourselves is the best way to make sure that happens. Plus, it helps us feel good, do well in school, and handle tough situations. And remember, self-care should be fun, too! So, find the things that you love to do and make sure to make time for them every day.

Taking care of yourself isn't something you should feel selfish about. It's just as important as taking care of others. After all, you can't pour from an empty cup. Fill your own cup first, and you'll have plenty to share with others. That's the magic of self-care!

Activity: Design Your Ideal Self-Care Day

Objective: The purpose of this activity is to help children understand what self-care means to them and how it can be incorporated into their daily lives. It encourages them to be creative and to think about their own needs and interests.

Materials needed:

- A blank sheet of paper

- Colored pencils, markers, or crayons

- Stickers, if desired

- A list of potential self-care activities for inspiration (optional)

Instructions:

1. **Brainstorming:** Start by thinking about what makes you feel good. What are the activities that you enjoy and that help you relax? This could include anything from reading a book, to going for a walk, to playing with your pet, to taking a warm bath.

2. **Visualizing the Day:** Next, imagine what your ideal day would look like from the moment you wake up until you go to bed. What self-care activities would you include? Remember, self-care isn't just about relaxing - it's also about taking care of your body and mind. This might include healthy meals, time for exercise, and plenty of sleep.

3. **Drawing the Day:** On your sheet of paper, start to draw your ideal self-care day. You can make this a timeline, a comic strip, or any other format that helps you visualize your day. Be creative and colorful!

4. **Reflecting:** Once you've drawn your day, take a moment to reflect on it. How do you feel when you imagine this day? Are there any activities you can start including in your real-life routine? This doesn't mean you need to do all these

activities every day - just think about how you can add more self-care into your life.

Remember, there's no right or wrong way to do self-care. The most important thing is to do activities that make you feel happy and healthy. Your ideal self-care day might look very different from someone else's - and that's okay!

Discussion Questions:

- How did it feel to design your ideal self-care day?

- Which activities are you most excited about?

- How can you start incorporating some of these activities into your everyday life?

- Why do you think self-care is important?

This activity encourages kids to think critically about what self-care means to them and to make a plan for including more self-care activities in their lives. It's a fun, creative, and meaningful way to teach kids about the importance of taking care of themselves.

Exercise: Self-Care Plan Worksheet

Objective: The goal of this worksheet is to help you create a self-care plan that suits your needs and interests. It's important to remember that everyone's self-care plan will look different - there's no right or wrong way to take care of yourself!

Instructions:

1. **List Your Favorite Self-Care Activities:** Think about the activities that make you feel good and help you relax. Write down as many as you can think of. These might include things like reading, playing a sport, spending time with a pet, or even just taking a few deep breaths.

2. **Daily Self-Care Activities:** Now, think about the self-care activities that you can do every day. These might be smaller activities, like brushing your teeth, eating a healthy breakfast, or taking a few minutes to relax and breathe deeply. Write down at least three daily self-care activities that you can commit to doing.

3. **Weekly Self-Care Activities:** Next, think about the self-care activities that you might do once a week. These could be bigger activities, like going for a hike, having a movie night, or spending time on a hobby you love. Write down at least two weekly self-care activities that you can commit to doing.

4. **Emergency Self-Care Activities:** Finally, think about the self-care activities that you can turn to when you're feeling really stressed or upset. These are your "emergency" self-care activities. They should be things that you know will help you feel better, even if it's just a little bit. Write down at least two emergency self-care activities that you can use when you need them.

Remember, the goal is not to do all of these activities all the time. The goal is to have a plan that you can turn to when you need it, so you always know how you can take care of yourself. And remember - it's okay to change your plan if you need to. Self-care is all about doing what's best for you!

Discussion Questions:

- How does it feel to have a self-care plan?

- What do you think will be the most challenging part of sticking to your plan?

- What do you think will be the most rewarding part of sticking to your plan?

- How can you remind yourself to follow your self-care plan?

This exercise will give children a structured way to think about self-care and to create a plan that suits their needs and preferences. The goal is to help them understand that self-care is a regular and necessary part of life, not just something to turn to in times of stress.

DBT and Self-Care

Self-care is all about taking good care of ourselves. It's like how you need to water a plant and give it sunlight to help it grow. We need to take care of ourselves in the same way to be happy and healthy.

You might think self-care is only about brushing your teeth, eating your vegetables, and getting enough sleep (which are all very important!), but it's also about taking care of your feelings and thoughts. That's where DBT comes in!

In DBT, we learn about a super cool skill called mindfulness. Mindfulness means paying attention to what's happening right now. It can be as simple as noticing how soft your pet's fur feels, how the sun warms your skin, or how your favorite food tastes. Practicing mindfulness is a way of taking care of our minds.

Another part of DBT is learning how to handle big emotions. Sometimes, our feelings can be like a really windy storm inside us. DBT teaches us skills to calm that storm. It's kind of like having a cozy blanket to wrap around ourselves when we're feeling upset or overwhelmed.

DBT also teaches us how to communicate better with others. This means understanding other people's feelings, asking for what we need in a respectful way, and saying 'no' when something doesn't feel right. It's like learning how to play in a team where everyone is heard and respected.

Lastly, DBT helps us to balance accepting things as they are and working to change what we can. It's like if you're learning to ride a bike and you keep falling off. DBT helps us to understand that it's okay to fall (that's the acceptance part), but we also need to keep trying and practicing to get better (that's the change part).

So, you see, DBT and self-care go together like peanut butter and jelly! By using DBT skills, we are taking care of our minds, our feelings, and our relationships. It's like a super-powered form of self-care!

Activity: DBT Self-Care Routine

Objective: The aim of this activity is to help kids understand how DBT skills can be incorporated into their daily lives to improve their self-care routine.

Materials Needed: Paper, colored pencils, markers, or crayons.

Instructions:

1. **Mindfulness Moment**: Start the day with a small mindfulness exercise. On your paper, draw a picture of a peaceful place you would like to imagine during your mindfulness moment in the morning. It could be a beach, a garden, or even outer space!

2. **Emotion Check-In**: After you get home from school, take a moment to check in with your emotions. Draw a face on your paper showing the emotion you might feel. Then, draw a tool from your DBT toolbox that you can use if you're feeling upset or overwhelmed.

3. **Balancing Act**: Write or draw about one thing that you accepted about your day (like getting a difficult homework assignment) and one thing you changed (like deciding to ask for help with the homework).

4. **Self-Soothing Activity**: Think of one activity you enjoy that calms you down. It could be reading a book, listening to music, or playing with a pet. Draw this activity on your paper.

5. **Gratitude Practice**: Before going to bed, think of three things you are grateful for. Draw or write them down on your paper.

6. **Mindfulness Goodnight**: End the day with another small mindfulness moment. Draw a picture of a calming image you would like to imagine before going to sleep.

After you finish creating your DBT self-care routine, hang it up somewhere you will see it every day, like next to your bed or on your bedroom door.

Remember, these are just suggestions. You can choose the DBT skills that work best for you and create a self-care routine that fits your own needs.

This activity helps children visualize and plan a self-care routine that incorporates DBT skills, reinforcing the connection between DBT and self-care. By drawing or writing about the activities, they are more likely to remember and follow through with them.

Exercise: Self-Care and DBT Reflection

Objective: The aim of this exercise is to encourage kids to reflect on how they are using DBT skills as part of their self-care routine, and to identify areas where they might want to focus more attention.

Materials Needed: A journal or piece of paper, and a pen or pencil.

Instructions:

1. **Mindfulness**: Reflect on your mindfulness moments from the past week. Write about one moment that was particularly calming or interesting. What did you notice during this moment?

2. **Emotion Check-In**: Think back to your emotion check-ins this week. Write about a time when you felt a strong emotion. How did you handle it? Did you use any DBT skills to help you?

3. **Balancing Act**: Reflect on something you accepted and something you changed this week. Write about why you chose to accept one thing and work to change another. How did it make you feel?

4. **Self-Soothing Activity**: Write about your favorite self-soothing activity from this week. Why do you enjoy it? How does it help you calm down?

5. **Gratitude Practice**: Look back on the things you were grateful for this week. Choose one and write about why you're thankful for it.

6. **Improvements**: Reflect on your week and think about if there's anything you would like to do differently in your self-care routine. Write about one thing you want to improve or change, and how you plan to do it.

Remember, there are no right or wrong answers in this exercise! It's all about reflecting on your own experiences and finding ways to make your self-care routine even better.

By reflecting on their experiences, children can become more aware of their emotions, their use of DBT skills, and their self-care practices. This reflection can support their understanding and mastery of DBT skills and encourage their continued growth and development.

CHAPTER 9: DEALING WITH DIFFICULT SITUATIONS

Understanding Difficult Situations

Life is full of adventures, and just like in any adventure, sometimes we come across challenging paths or tough puzzles. We call these "difficult situations." They might feel like trying to solve a super tricky math problem or like being lost in a maze. But don't worry! Just like any puzzle, these difficult situations can also be solved.

Imagine you're playing a game of basketball, and suddenly, the ball gets stuck in a tree. That's a difficult situation, right? You can't reach it, and you can't play without it. But what do you do? You don't just stand there, do you? No, you try to figure out ways to get the ball down - maybe by using a long stick, or by shaking the tree trunk.

Life's difficult situations are just like that basketball stuck in the tree. They might be problems with your homework, disagreements with friends, or feeling really upset or worried about something. These situations can make you feel stuck, just like that basketball. But remember, there is always a way to unstick that ball!

It's normal to feel a little scared or upset when you're in a difficult situation. It might feel like a big, dark cloud is hanging over your head. But just like every cloud has a silver lining, every difficult situation has a solution. Sometimes, we just need to think and try different things until we find the solution. And sometimes, we might need to ask for help, and that's perfectly okay!

Understanding difficult situations means realizing that they are a part of life, just like sunny days and rainy days. And just like we use an umbrella to keep dry on rainy days, we can use our minds and hearts to find solutions to our problems.

Remember, difficult situations help us learn and grow. When we solve a tricky math problem, we become better at math, right? Similarly, when we find our way out of a difficult situation, we become better problem-solvers. We learn about ourselves, about others, and about the world.

So the next time you face a difficult situation, don't be scared. Think of it as a tricky puzzle waiting to be solved, a basketball stuck in a tree that you can definitely get down. Take a deep breath, think about what you can do, and don't be afraid to ask for help. You're smarter and stronger than you think, and you can handle any difficult situation that comes your way!

And always remember, just like the sun always shines after the rain, there are always good times after difficult situations. So keep your chin up, and keep going!

Activity: Problem-Solving Role Play

Objective: To help kids understand how to tackle difficult situations through problem-solving techniques using role play.

Materials Needed:

- Index cards with different difficult situations written on them

- A hat or bowl to draw the cards from

Instructions:

1. **Prepare the Scenario Cards:** Before the activity begins, write down several different difficult scenarios on the index cards. The scenarios should be relatable to the kids' everyday life. For example:

    - "Your best friend borrowed your favorite book and lost it."

    - "You have a big project due tomorrow, and you haven't started."

    - "Your sibling broke your toy, and they won't admit it."

2. **Introduce the Activity:** Explain to the kids that they will be acting out different scenarios and coming up with ways to solve the problems in those scenarios.

3. **Divide into Pairs:** Divide the kids into pairs. Each pair will have a chance to role-play a scenario.

4. **Draw a Scenario:** One pair will draw a card from the hat or bowl and read the scenario aloud.

5. **Role Play:** The kids will then role-play the scenario. One will play the person facing the problem, and the other will play a helpful friend, family member, or teacher.

6. **Brainstorm Solutions:** The kids will act out the problem, then pause and brainstorm possible solutions. They should discuss and consider different approaches to the problem.

7. **Act Out the Solution:** Once they've decided on a solution, they'll act out implementing it in the role-play.

8. **Discussion:** After each pair finishes their role play, have a group discussion about the problem and solution. What did they think about the solution? Could there have been other solutions? What could they learn from this scenario?

This activity encourages kids to think critically and creatively about problem-solving. By acting out the scenarios, they're able to better understand the problems and the impact of different solutions. Plus, it's a lot of fun!

Exercise: Difficult Situations Scenario Worksheet

Objective: To provide kids with the opportunity to practice problem-solving skills in written form using various scenarios.

Materials Needed:

- Printable scenario worksheets

- Pens or pencils

Instructions for the Worksheet:

The worksheet will contain several scenarios that represent difficult situations. Here are some examples of scenarios you could include:

1. **Scenario:** You're playing in the park and find a lost puppy with no collar or tags. What would you do?

2. **Scenario:** You're at school and see a classmate being bullied. How would you handle this situation?

3. **Scenario:** Your friend tells a lie about you to other friends. How would you address this?

4. **Scenario:** You have a big test tomorrow, but you also have a soccer match this evening. How would you manage your time?

5. **Scenario:** Your younger sibling goes into your room and breaks your favorite toy. How would you react?

For each scenario, ask the following questions:

1. **Describe the Problem:** What is the main issue or problem in this scenario?

2. **Brainstorm Solutions:** What are two different ways you could respond to this situation?

3. **Consider Consequences:** For each solution, what do you think would happen next? What might be the result of each action?

4. **Choose a Solution:** Based on your thoughts, which solution do you think is the best? Why?

5. **Reflect:** How do you feel about your decision? Do you think it would be easy or hard to do this in real life? Why?

This worksheet can be a great tool for encouraging kids to think through problems step-by-step and consider the potential consequences of their actions. It's also a great way for them to practice empathy and decision-making skills.

DBT Skills for Difficult Situations

Did you know that our brains are like superheroes? Just like superheroes have different powers to solve different problems, our brains have different skills they can use when things get tough. In DBT (which is short for Dialectical Behavior Therapy), we learn about some really cool skills that can help us when we face difficult situations.

Imagine you're playing a video game, and you encounter a tough level that you just can't seem to beat. It's frustrating, right? But what if you had a special tool or power-up that could help you get through that level? DBT skills are like those power-ups. They can help us "level up" in real life when we face challenging situations.

One of the most important skills in DBT is called 'distress tolerance'. It's a big phrase, but it's not as complicated as it sounds. 'Distress' is a fancy word for feeling upset or stressed out, and 'tolerance' means being able to handle it. So, distress tolerance is all about handling tough feelings without letting them control us. It's like having a super-shield that helps us face scary monsters in our video game.

Then, there's 'emotional regulation'. This is another superpower that helps us change how we feel when we're upset. It's like having a magic wand that can turn a fire-breathing dragon into a friendly puppy. Emotional regulation can help us calm down when we're feeling really angry or cheer up when we're feeling sad.

The last power-up we'll talk about today is 'interpersonal effectiveness'. This sounds fancy, but it's just about being good at talking to others. It helps us ask for what we want in a nice way, say no when we need to, and keep our friends even when we disagree. It's like having a power-up that helps us make more friends and allies in our game.

Remember, everyone faces difficult levels in their life game. Sometimes, we might feel scared, upset, or angry, and that's okay. What's important is that we have our DBT power-ups ready. With them, we can face any tough situation that comes our way.

And the best part? Just like in a video game, the more we practice using these skills, the better we get at them. So, keep practicing your DBT skills, and you'll become a real-life superhero in no time!

Activity: Crisis Survival Kit Creation

Objective: To create a personal "Crisis Survival Kit" that can be used to practice DBT skills during difficult situations.

Materials Needed:

- A small box or bag (this will be the "kit")

- Paper and pens or markers

- Any other items the child finds comforting (like a soft toy, a favorite book, etc.)

Instructions:

1. **Introduction:** Explain to the kids that everyone sometimes faces difficult situations or big feelings that can be hard to manage. This "Crisis Survival Kit" will be a tool they can use when they need a little extra help.

2. **Choose the Container:** Let the kids choose a small box or bag that they like. This will become their personal "Crisis Survival Kit". They can decorate it however they want!

3. **Create a List of DBT Skills:** On a piece of paper, have the kids write down some DBT skills that they find helpful. These might include deep breathing for mindfulness, a phrase that reminds them of distress tolerance, or an idea for how to regulate their emotions. This list will go in the kit as a reminder of the tools they have available.

4. **Add Comforting Items:** Next, let the kids add items to the kit that they find comforting or helpful. This could be a favorite small toy, a comforting blanket, or even a favorite book. These items can help provide comfort during a difficult moment.

5. **Practice Using the Kit:** Once the kit is assembled, have the kids practice using it. They can pretend they're in a challenging situation, and use the items

in the kit to help them manage their feelings. This practice can help them feel more comfortable using the kit when they really need it.

6. **Reflect:** After the practice, have a discussion with the kids about how it felt to use the kit. Did they find it helpful? Would they like to add or remove anything? The kit can be adjusted as needed to best suit each child's needs.

Wrap-up: Remind the kids that everyone faces tough situations, but with their new Crisis Survival Kits, they have a set of tools ready to help them navigate these challenges. Encourage them to use their kits whenever they need to and to keep practicing their DBT skills.

This activity not only helps kids understand DBT concepts in a practical way, but it also gives them a tangible tool they can use when they're feeling upset or overwhelmed. It's a great way to make DBT skills more accessible and actionable for kids.

Exercise: Problem-Solving with DBT Skills Practice

Objective: To practice using DBT skills in problem-solving scenarios.

Materials Needed:

- Problem-Solving Worksheet

- Pencil or Pen

Instructions:

1. **Introduction:** Explain to the kids that sometimes, life gives us problems that can seem hard to solve. But with our DBT skills, we can figure out the best way to handle these situations.

2. **Problem-Solving Scenarios:** Provide the kids with a worksheet that has several hypothetical scenarios. Here are a few examples:

   - Scenario 1: You're working on a group project for school, but one of your teammates isn't doing their part. How can you handle this situation using your DBT skills?

   - Scenario 2: You're at the park and some kids you don't know start making fun of you. What DBT skills can you use to deal with this situation?

   - Scenario 3: You're really upset because your best friend moved away and you miss them a lot. Which DBT skills can help you manage your feelings?

3. **Response Time:** Give the kids some time to write down their responses to each scenario. They should try to identify which DBT skills they would use and describe how they would use them.

4. **Discussion:** Once everyone is done, have a discussion about the different responses. What DBT skills did the kids choose to use? Why did they think

these skills would be helpful? This can be a great way to reinforce the DBT skills and help the kids understand when to use each one.

Wrap-up: Remind the kids that problems are a normal part of life, but with their DBT skills, they have the tools they need to handle them. Encourage them to keep practicing their DBT skills and to use them when they face real-life problems.

This exercise allows the kids to practice applying DBT skills to hypothetical scenarios, which can help them feel more confident about using these skills in their own lives. It also encourages them to think critically about which skills are most appropriate for different situations.

CHAPTER 10: LIVING A BALANCED LIFE WITH DBT

Life balance might sound like a tricky idea, but it's really quite simple and super important. Just like how a tightrope walker needs to keep balanced to stay on the rope, we all need to keep balanced in our lives to stay happy and healthy.

Imagine you're riding on a see-saw. If one side is too heavy, you'll be stuck in the air. If the other side is too heavy, you'll be stuck on the ground. But if you balance the weight, you can have a fun ride, going up and down smoothly. Life is a lot like that see-saw.

So, what does a balanced life look like? Well, it means spending the right amount of time on different parts of your life, like school, family, hobbies, rest, and friendships.

Think about your day like a big, delicious pie. If you only put one ingredient in the pie, it wouldn't taste very good, would it? A tasty pie needs a mix of different ingredients. Similarly, a balanced day needs a mix of different activities. You can't spend all day playing video games or all day doing homework. You need to mix it up with some family time, a little bit of chores, some rest, and, of course, some fun!

Keeping a balanced life also means paying attention to your feelings and needs. Sometimes, we might feel stressed or tired. That's okay. It's our body's way of telling us we need to slow down, rest a bit, or do something fun. Other times, we might feel super energetic and ready to take on the world. That's great too! It's all about listening to what our bodies and minds are telling us.

Life balance doesn't mean that everything has to be perfect all the time. We all have good days and not-so-good days, and that's okay. The important thing is to try to make sure that over time, we're not doing too much of one thing and not enough of another.

Remember, balancing is not about being still; it's about moving and adjusting. Just like a dancer, we need to move and adjust to keep our balance in life. If we spend too much time on one thing, we can adjust by spending a little more time on something else.

Life balance is all about making sure we have a 'just right' mixture of everything we do and feel. And just like learning to ride a bike or tie your shoelaces, it might take some practice to get the hang of it, but once you do, it'll be a breeze!

Remember, you're the best judge of your own balance. Listen to your heart, your mind, and your body. They'll help you find your perfect balance.

Activity: Life Balance Collage

Activity: Life Balance Collage

Objective: To help children visualize and understand the concept of a balanced life.

Materials Needed:

1. A large piece of poster board or construction paper

2. Old magazines, newspapers, or printouts

3. Scissors

4. Glue

5. Markers or colored pencils

Instructions:

1. **Explain the Activity:** Start by explaining to the kids what a collage is (a piece of art made by sticking various different materials such as photographs and pieces of paper or fabric onto a backing). Let them know that they will be creating a "Life Balance Collage" that represents all the different parts of their life.

2. **Brainstorming:** Ask the kids to think about all the different parts of their lives that are important to them. This could include school, family, friends, hobbies, sports, relaxation, chores, and more. Write down these categories on the board or a piece of paper.

3. **Collect Images:** Next, have the kids go through the magazines, newspapers, or printouts and cut out pictures that represent these different areas of their life. For example, they might cut out a picture of a family having dinner for "Family Time," or a picture of a bed for "Rest."

4. **Create the Collage:** Once they have collected enough images, they can start arranging and gluing them onto their poster board or construction paper. They should try to balance the different areas of their life in their collage. For

instance, if they only have one picture related to school but ten pictures related to video games, they might need to find more school-related pictures to create a more balanced collage.

5. **Discuss the Collage:** After the collages are complete, have the kids present their collages to the group. They can explain why they chose the pictures they did and how it represents balance in their life.

Wrap-Up: Remind the kids that just like their collages, a balanced life has a bit of everything. And it's okay if some days don't seem perfectly balanced, what's important is that over time, they're making space for all the important parts of their lives.

This activity is not only fun but also a great way to visually represent the concept of life balance. It can help kids understand that a balanced life includes a variety of activities and experiences.

Exercise: Life Balance Reflection

Exercise: Life Balance Reflection

Objective: To encourage children to think about their own lives and how they can maintain a balanced lifestyle.

Materials Needed:

1. "Life Balance Reflection" worksheet

2. Pen or pencil

Instructions:

1. **Introduce the Exercise:** Let the kids know that they are going to think about their own lives and how they might balance different activities and aspects of their lives.

2. **Hand Out the Worksheet:** The worksheet should have the following sections:

   - **School:** How much time do you spend on schoolwork? Do you think you need to spend more or less time on it?

   - **Family:** How often do you spend quality time with your family? How can you make sure you are spending enough time with them?

   - **Friends:** How often do you play or hang out with friends? Do you need more or less friend time?

   - **Hobbies:** What hobbies do you enjoy? Are you able to spend enough time on them?

   - **Rest:** How much time do you spend relaxing, or doing nothing at all? Do you need more rest?

   - **Physical Activity:** How often do you do physical activities like sports or playing outside? Do you need to do more or less?

- **Chores:** How much time do you spend doing chores? Is it too much or too little?

3. **Reflect and Write:** Give the kids some time to reflect on these questions and write down their thoughts in each section.

4. **Group Discussion:** Once everyone has finished, you can invite the kids to share their reflections if they feel comfortable. This can be a good opportunity for them to learn from each other's insights.

Wrap-Up: Remind the children that everyone's balance will look different and that's perfectly okay. What's important is that they are aware of their own needs and are working towards their own version of a balanced life.

DBT for a Balanced Life

When we think about balance, we might imagine a seesaw or a tightrope walker at a circus. In both cases, everything needs to be just right, or else the seesaw tips over or the tightrope walker falls. Life is a lot like that, too! Having a balanced life means doing a little bit of everything we love and need. It's like making a colorful life-salad with different ingredients like schoolwork, playtime, family time, rest, and hobbies.

Dialectical Behavior Therapy, or DBT as we like to call it, can help us create this balanced life-salad. Just like how a good salad has different ingredients, DBT has different skills. These skills help us handle our feelings, work well with others, and make it through tough times without tipping our life-seesaw too much.

The first skill is mindfulness. This is like the salad bowl that holds all our life ingredients together. Being mindful means paying attention to what's happening right now. It's like when you're eating your favorite ice cream, and you notice its creamy texture and sweet taste. Mindfulness helps us appreciate the good moments and deal better with the not-so-good ones.

Then, we have distress tolerance. Imagine if you suddenly found a bug in your salad - yuck! Distress tolerance is like the fork that helps us pick out this bug and move on. It's about surviving and accepting life's unpleasant parts without letting them ruin our whole day.

Emotional regulation is another important skill. It's like the dressing that makes our salad taste just right. This skill helps us manage our feelings so they don't get too big or too small. If we feel too excited or too upset, it's hard to enjoy our life-salad. Emotional regulation helps us keep our feelings in check.

Interpersonal effectiveness is like knowing how to share our salad with others. It's about communicating well and maintaining good relationships. This skill helps us ask for what we need, say no when we want to, and still keep our friends and family happy.

Lastly, we have the balance between acceptance and change. Sometimes, we have to accept things as they are, like if it's raining and we can't go out to play. Other times, we can make changes, like doing indoor activities instead. Knowing when to accept and when to change is like knowing when our salad needs more tomatoes or less lettuce.

Activity: Design Your Balanced Life with DBT

Objective: This activity will help kids understand how to use DBT skills to create a balanced life. They will create a visual representation, using the metaphor of a "life-salad" to represent the different parts of their lives.

Materials Needed:

- Large piece of paper or poster board

- Markers or colored pencils

- Magazines, scissors, and glue (optional, for a collage-style activity)

Instructions:

1. **Brainstorm Different Life Areas:** Start by thinking about the different parts of your life, like school, family, friends, hobbies, rest, and chores. Write these down on a piece of paper. These are the ingredients of your life-salad.

2. **Create Your Life-Salad Bowl:** On your large piece of paper or poster board, draw a big bowl. This is your life-salad bowl, and it represents your life as a whole.

3. **Add Your Life Ingredients:** Now, draw or write each part of your life from step 1 into your salad bowl. You could draw pictures, write words, or cut out images from magazines. Try to think about how much of each ingredient you have in your life right now. If you spend a lot of time on schoolwork, that ingredient might take up a big part of your salad.

4. **Think About Balance:** Look at your life-salad. Is it balanced? Do you have too much of one ingredient and not enough of another? Maybe you have a lot of schoolwork but not enough rest or playtime. Draw or write what you would like more or less of in your salad.

5. **Apply DBT Skills:** Now think about how you can use DBT skills to make your life-salad more balanced. Here are some ideas:

- Mindfulness: Could you spend some time each day paying attention to the present moment?

- Distress Tolerance: What could you do when you find a "bug" in your salad, like a problem or tough situation?

- Emotional Regulation: How could you manage your feelings to make your salad taste just right?

- Interpersonal Effectiveness: How could you communicate better or build stronger relationships?

- Acceptance and Change: What parts of your life do you need to accept, and what parts can you change?

6. **Make a Plan:** Based on your thoughts from step 5, make a plan for how you can use DBT skills to improve your life balance. Write or draw this plan next to your life-salad. This could include specific things you'll do, like practicing mindfulness every morning or using distress tolerance when you're upset.

Remember, it's okay if your life-salad isn't perfect. It's yours, and you can always change it up with the help of DBT skills. And just like making a salad, it takes practice to make a balanced life. So, let's keep practicing together!

Exercise: Personal DBT Goal Setting

Objective: This exercise is designed to help kids apply what they've learned about DBT to their own lives. They will set personal goals related to each of the main DBT skills: mindfulness, distress tolerance, emotional regulation, interpersonal effectiveness, and the balance between acceptance and change.

Materials Needed:

- A piece of paper or a journal

- Pen or pencil

Instructions:

1. **Reflect on DBT Skills:** Start by thinking about each of the DBT skills you've learned about: mindfulness, distress tolerance, emotional regulation, interpersonal effectiveness, and the balance between acceptance and change. Reflect on what each skill means to you and why it's important.

2. **Write a Goal for Each DBT Skill:** Now, write a personal goal for each of the DBT skills. This should be something specific and achievable that you can work on. Here are some examples:

   - Mindfulness: "I will practice mindfulness for 5 minutes each day after school."

   - Distress Tolerance: "When I'm feeling upset, I will use my distress tolerance skills before reacting."

   - Emotional Regulation: "I will use my emotional regulation skills to manage my anger when I'm feeling frustrated."

   - Interpersonal Effectiveness: "I will use my interpersonal effectiveness skills to express my needs in a respectful way to my friends and family."

- Acceptance and Change: "I will practice accepting things I can't change and working to change things I can."

3. **Create a Plan to Achieve Your Goals:** Next, create a plan for how you're going to achieve each of your goals. This could include specific steps you'll take, people who can support you, or resources you can use. For example, if your goal is to practice mindfulness each day, your plan might include setting a reminder on your phone or choosing a quiet spot where you can practice without being disturbed.

4. **Check-In On Your Progress:** Finally, decide how and when you'll check in on your progress. This could be once a week, once a month, or whatever works best for you. During each check-in, reflect on how you're doing with your goals and make any necessary adjustments to your plan.

Remember, it's okay if you don't meet your goals right away. Just like learning any new skill, it takes practice to get better at using DBT skills. The important thing is to keep trying and to be kind to yourself along the way. You're already taking a big step by setting these goals, and you should be proud of yourself for that!

CONCLUSION

Dear young explorers, we've reached the end of our journey through the 'Essential DBT Workbook for Kids Aged 8-12'. What an adventure we've had together! You've done such an amazing job, learning new things, participating in activities, and completing exercises. But remember, even though we've reached the end of this book, your adventure with DBT is just beginning.

DBT is a very special toolbox filled with helpful skills. These are not just any skills, but superpowers that can help you navigate the ups and downs of life. You've learnt about mindfulness, emotional regulation, distress tolerance, and interpersonal effectiveness. It might seem like a lot, but guess what? You're now equipped with tools to help you understand and manage your emotions, tolerate distress, interact effectively with others, and live a balanced life.

Mindfulness, the first skill we learned, is like a super telescope. It helps us to see and experience the present moment clearly. By practicing mindfulness, you can enjoy every scoop of your favorite ice cream, listen to a friend's story with full attention, and even feel the breeze on your face more vividly. Isn't it amazing how mindfulness helps us appreciate the simple joys of life?

Then we discovered the power of emotional regulation. It's like a superhero's shield, helping you manage and respond to your feelings in a healthy way. Now, when you're feeling sad, angry, or even super excited, you know how to handle these emotions. You can use your shield to protect yourself and others from emotional storms.

We also learned about distress tolerance. This is your superhero strength, helping you endure difficult situations without losing control. So when things get tough, you can summon your inner strength, just like a superhero, and make it through.

And don't forget about interpersonal effectiveness. These are your superhero communication skills. They help you talk to others, make friends, ask for what you need, and say no when necessary. With these skills, you can build stronger relationships and understand others better.

In the chapters on acceptance and change, self-care, dealing with difficult situations, and living a balanced life, you learned how all these skills come together. They're like your superhero team, always ready to help you make the best of every situation.

Now, it's important to remember that every superhero needs practice to master their powers. The same goes for your new DBT skills. Don't worry if you don't get everything perfect right away. With time and practice, you'll get better and better. So, keep using your workbook, repeat the activities, and continue to learn and grow.

Remember, just like superheroes, everyone has their unique strengths and weaknesses, and that's okay. It's what makes us special. The most important thing is that you continue to try your best, learn from your experiences, and never stop growing.

You're already a hero for completing this workbook. Keep your DBT tools handy and use them whenever you need. Remember, you have everything you need inside you to face whatever life brings your way. So go forth, young superheroes, and remember that every challenge is an opportunity for you to shine.

Thank you for embarking on this DBT journey. I'm incredibly proud of you and all the progress you've made. Here's to your continued journey of growth, learning, and discovery. Keep shining, keep learning, and keep being the amazing you!

Made in the USA
Monee, IL
04 October 2023

43968153R00077